HOW & WHY KEY WORDS CONTROL YOUR LIFE!

Plus Historical & Cultural Facts
About America,
China, Japan, Korea and India!

KEY WORDS CONTROL YOUR LIFE!

Two things are infinite: the universe and human stupidity; and I'm not sure about the universe.

—Albert Einstein—

HOW & WHY Key Words Control Your Life!

Plus Historical & Cultural Facts about America, China, Japan, Korea and India!

Boyè Lafayette De Mente

A PHOENIX BOOKS ORIGINAL

Copyright © 2014 by
Boyè Lafayette De Mente

KEY WORDS CONTROL YOUR LIFE!

Other Books by the Author

[Books on China]

The Chinese Mind—Understanding Traditional Chinese
Beliefs and their Influence
on Contemporary Culture that
Reveal the Culture and Mindset of the Chinese]

Chinese in Plain English

Survival Chinese & Instant Chinese

Etiquette Guide to China—Know the Rules that
Make the Difference

CHINA – Understanding & Dealing with the Chinese Way
of Doing Business

[Books on Japan]

JAPAN – Understanding & Dealing with the New
Japanese Way of Doing Business

KATA—The Key to Understanding & Dealing
With the Japanese

Japan's Cultural Code Words

The Japanese Have a Word for It!

Mistress-Keeping in Japan

Exotic Japan—The Sensual & Visual Pleasures

Discovering Cultural Japan

Business Guide to Japan

Japanese in Plain English

KEY WORDS CONTROL YOUR LIFE!

Speak Japanese Today—A Little Language Goes a Long Way!

Instant Japanese & Survival Japanese

Japan Made Easy—All You Need to Know to Enjoy Japan

Dining Guide to Japan

Shopping Guide to Japan

Etiquette Guide to Japan—Know the Rules that Make the Difference

The Japanese Samurai Code—Classic Strategies for Success

Japan Unmasked—The Character & Culture of the Japanese

Elements of Japanese Design—Understanding & Using Japan's Classic *Wabi-Sabi-Shibui* Concepts

Sex and the Japanese—The Sensual Side of Japan

Samurai Strategies—42 Secret Martial Arts from Musashi's "Book of Five Rings"

Why the Japanese are a Superior People—The Advantages of Using Both Sides of Your Brain!

Amazing Japan—Why Japan is one of the World's Most Intriguing Countries

Exotic Japan—The Sensual & Visual Pleasures

SABURO—The Saga of a Teenage Samurai in 17th Century Japan

KEY WORDS CONTROL YOUR LIFE!

THE KATA FACTOR! Japan's Secret Weapon!

[Books on Korea]

Korean Business Etiquette

Korean in Plain English

Korea's Business & Cultural Code Words

Etiquette Guide to Korea— Know the Rules that Make the Difference

Instant Korean / Survival Korean

[Books on Mexico]

Why Mexicans Think & Behave the Way They Do— The Cultural Factors that Created the Character & Personality of the Mexican People

THE MEXICAN MIND – Understanding & Appreciating Mexican Culture

Romantic Mexico—The Image & the Realities

[Other Titles]

Which Side of Your Brain Am I Talking To? – The Advantages of Using Both Sides of Your Brain

How to Measure the Sexuality of Men & Women by Their Facial Features

Samurai Principles & Practices that will Help Preteens & Teens in School, Sports, Social Activities & Choosing Careers

Romantic Hawaii—Sun, Sand, Surf & Sex

KEY WORDS CONTROL YOUR LIFE!

Women of the Orient

Asian Face Reading—Unlock the Secrets Hidden in the Human Face

Why Ignorance, Stupidity and Violence Plague Mankind

How to Measure the Sexuality of Men & Women by Their Facial Features

Bridging Cultural Barriers in China, Japan, Korea & Mexico

BRAVE NEW WORLD OF AMERICAN SEX!

THE PLAGUE OF MALE DOMINANCE The Cause & the Cure!

THE ORIGINS OF HUMAN VIOLENCE! – Male Dominance, Ignorance, Religions & Willful Stupidity!

WHY ORIENTAL GIRLS ATTRACT WESTERN MEN!

ONCE A FOOL—From Japan to Alaska by Amphibious Jeep

*All of these titles are available from Amazon

**Some of the Japan titles are also available in Chinese, Czech, French, German, Hebrew, Italian, Indonesian, Japanese, Polish, Portuguese, Russian & Spanish editions.*

KEY WORDS CONTROL YOUR LIFE!

CONTENTS

THE ROLE OF LANGUAGES IN HUMAN BEHAVIOR

AMERICAN ENGLISH REVEALS CULTURAL INSIGHTS!
Key Words Define the American Mindset

CHINA'S LANGUAGES REVEAL CULTURAL INSIGHTS!
Ten of the Most Important Words in Mandarin

THE JAPANESE LANGUAGE REVEALS CULTURAL INSIGHTS!
Ten of the Most Important Words in Japanese

THE KOREAN LANGUAGE REVEALS CULTURAL INSIGHTS!
Ten of the Most Important Words in Korean

ASPECTS OF AMERICA, CHINA, JAPAN, KOREA & INDIA

COMMUNICATING IN JAPANESE!
HIGH-TECH SENSE OF THE JAPANESE
Catching Up with Star Trek!
Getting Off the Beaten Track!
Amazing Facts About Japan!
Japan's Shogun Era Only a Doorway Away!
Visitors Can Learn About Japan's Amazing Ninja!

KEY WORDS CONTROL YOUR LIFE!

Japanese Girls Going After Geeks & Nerds!
Japan's Amazing High-Tech Factory-Farms
Saving the Sexy "Cover-It-All-Up" Kimono
Understand the Yugen Element in the Beauty
Of Japanese Arts & Crafts
Innovations, Inventions Changing the
"Samurai" Lifestyle
New Elements Adding to the Ambiance
Of Life in Japan!
Secrets of Japan's Appeal to Westerners
Japanese Scientists Copying Nature!
Places to Go if You Think
You Have "Seen" Japan
The Exotic Orient
A Remarkable People-Future-Oriented
Enterprise
Getting Taken for a Ride in Japan!
Cultural Ways of Pleasuring in the
Brevity of Life!
The Changes in Meeting & Mating in Japan!
Japan's New "Marriage Hunt" Phenomena!
Getting off of the Beaten Track and
Having a Spiritual Experience!
The Fascinating Story of Inns in Japan!
Japan Has Had a Tourism Industry
For 2,000 years!
Viewing Japan from the Top of the World!
An Only in Japan Kind of Thing!
Branch of Tokyo SkyTree Sprouts
Beer Pubs
High-Tech Advances Turn Toilets
Into Suites Fit for Royalty!

KEY WORDS CONTROL YOUR LIFE!

THE END OF THE GOD MYTH!
The One-God Concept
Jews Create Yahweh/God
The Jesus Christ Add-On
The Spread of Christianity
God's Terrible Swift Sword!
The Power of the God Cult
Promoting and Selling God
If Gods Were Actually in Charge!
Sex in Godless Societies
Sex around the World
How Males Put a Kink in the Sex Life
Of Both Sexes!
How to Select Hot Mates Instead
Of Cold Fish!
Mexico's Seductive Lifestyle!
Why Oriental Girls Attract Western Men!
World's Cultures Mired in the Muck
Of Ignorance, Stupidity and Violence!
THE NEW GOD!
The Rise of Money Morality
THE REAL GODS OF THE COSMOS
The Nature of Nature

MOTHER INDIA!
An Astounding Historical Debt Most People
Know Nothing About!
The Origin of Buddhism in India
The Roots of Chinese Civilization

KEY WORDS CONTROL YOUR LIFE!

THE ROLE OF LANGUAGES IN HUMAN BEHAVIOR

AMERICAN ENGLISH

American English has altogether different roots than other languages of the world because the factors responsible for its development are totally different from those that gave birth to other languages.

The original European Americans came to the Amercan continent from England to escape the limits and bonds imposed upon them by a patriarchal government and the Church of England..

The first major contributors to American English were the well educated, the scholars, and the writers of the day…the founders of the country and its ethos.

The American Constitution mandates that life, liberty and the pursuit of happiness are inalienable rights of all Americans.

The American mindset and the behavior that resulted from this declaration left it up to individuals to decide on their own how they would think and behave, and that meant the environment that children were born and raised it created and controlled their mindset and behavior. There was very little formal education in the first generations of Americans.

The policies established by the founders of the first American colonies did not take into account the

KEY WORDS CONTROL YOUR LIFE!

genetic differences in the brain power or the personality and character of individuals.

Americans therefore became the most freethinking and freewheeling people on the planet. Parents set the rules for their children based on their own perceptions of good and bad behavior.. Schools and other organizations had their own rules of behavior.

There was no precise set of cultural-bound rules similar to those that developed in India, China and Korea. Each person reacted to the factors that influenced his or her home life and education.

About the only general yardstick was the religious-based concept of right-and-wrong, and this varied a great deal, especially with males.

When the Japanese first encountered Americans they complained that they were all liars and could not be trusted or depended on.

Many of the "key words" in the American vocabulary—freedom, liberty, independence, individualism, personal ambition—and so on were meaningless to most Asians.

Because of this the Chinese, Japanese and Koreans historically claimed that Americans were hard to anticipate, to predict.

KEY WORDS CONTROL YOUR LIFE!

RETURN OF THE CHINESE DRAGON!

After some 500 years of dormancy the Chinese dragon is back. And as I have been saying since the mid-1990s, Americans had better learn how to level the playing field with China or how to shine shoes.

CHINA'S LANGUAGES REVEAL CULTUAL INSIGHTS

There are a dozen or more fundamental elements of Chinese culture that make it different from Western cultures, but just one of these elements provides deep insight into the differences in their mindset and behavior.

This one element is the use of *Han zi* (Hahn-jee), literally meaning "Chinese characters," which the Chinese and the Japanese and Koreans] have traditionally used to transcribe their languages. [The better known Japanese version of this designation is *Kahn ji* [Kahn jee]…and generally both *Han zi* and *Kan ji* are written as one word when transcribed into Roman letters.]

Hanzi originated in China between five and six thousand years ago and eventually numbered around 250,000 characters—a number that was gradually pared down over the millennia, and is now around 5,000 for scholars and from 4,000 to 2,000 for ordinary people.

KEY WORDS CONTROL YOUR LIFE!

All *Hanzi* are based on the stylization of concepts, objects and other things from real life. In other words, they are "pictures" of things that have inherent meanings. They are not just substitutes for sounds as in the Roman alphabet.

Furthermore, unlike the simple Roman alphabet, Chinese characters consist of one to as many as thirty or more individual "strokes" that must "fit" together, and by long tradition must be drawn in a precise order.

The Chinese *Hanzi* system of writing was impo-sed on Koreans more than two thousand years ago and was adopted by the Japanese between the 6th and 7th centuries A.D.

By 1,000 B.C. one of the key measurements of the cultural achievements of educated Chinese was how many of the characters they could read and write. As time went by how artistically they could render the characters as *shufa* (shuu-fah) or calligraphy became more and more important.

This same phenomenon occurred in both Korea and Japan, with the greatest calligraphy masters becoming historical icons who are still remembered and celebrated today.

By the 1700s even Japan's notorious samurai warriors took as much pride in their ability to draw *Kanji* as calligraphy, known as *shodō* [show-dohh] in Japanese, as they did in their skill in drawing and using their deadly swords.

KEY WORDS CONTROL YOUR LIFE!

The point of this is that learning how to read and draw large numbers of the intricate *Hanzi* has had a profound influence on the mindset and manual skills of the Chinese, Japanese and Korean since ancient times.

Still today from their earliest years in kindergarten and elementary schools, learning how to draw some two thousand ideograms forces them to focus with laser-like intensity on the characters and to develop eye-and-hand coordination that influences the rest of their lives.

Learning to read and draw the ideograms requires not only intense concentration but perseverance, acute concern with the finest details and an appreciation for form, harmony and function—all characteristics that are associated with the mindset of adult Chinese, Japanese and Koreans in all of their affairs, from meticulous planning in business to scientific research.

Westerners, on the other hand, are expected to learn how to pronounce the sounds and to draw only twenty-six letters that by themselves have no meaning. This alone accounts for much of the contrast between the academic prowess of Westerners and their Chinese, Japanese and Korean counterparts.

Another important contrast between Westerners and *Han*zi-influenced Asians is that popular Western culture—American culture in particular—now de-emphasizes long periods of concentration and meticulous effort in favor of speed and superficiality in

KEY WORDS CONTROL YOUR LIFE!

everything, from education to manufacturing and entertainment.

This is a cultural weakness that threatens the future of the United States and other Western countries, and is a barrier that cannot be eliminated in a short time because it has become an inseparable part of the mindset and lifestyle of most Westerners.

Until well into the 20th century educated Europeans and Americans at least learned how to write the Roman alphabet clearly and often beautifully. Now, even mediocre handwriting appears to be on its way out.

I am not proposing that Americans and other Westerners learn how to transcribe their languages in Chinese ideograms, but unless we act to upgrade the level of our culture we will continue to be at a disadvantage in dealing with people programmed by their intense exposure to *Hanzi*.

There are, of course, links between the languages of the West that evolved from or were influenced by the Latin language, spread across much of Western Europe by the Roman Empire.

These Latin links have significantly influenced the cultures they merged with. But even Latin-linked cultures that are as close as American and British have language-based differences that are profound, and if not taken into consideration can—and do—lead to misunderstandings and gaps in cross-cultural communication.

KEY WORDS CONTROL YOUR LIFE!

It has been proven time and again that a gap in communication of less than one percent can eventually lead to serious problems if not recognized and remedied in a timely manner.

To understand and appreciate the role and importance of *Hanzi* in Chinese culture one would have to imagine that all of the European societies that came under the influence of the Roman Empire adopted the written form of Latin to transcribe their languages but retained much of their own system of pronunciation.

That is exactly what happened among China's fifty-three ethic groups that originally had and still have the own languages. Twenty-three of these minority groups had their own writing systems.

Over centuries, these diverse groups of people gradually adopted *Hanzi* to write their languages. They retained the meanings of the individual characters but they pronounced them in their original language. This meant that virtually all Chinese who were literate, regardless of their native tongue, could communicate with each other in writing, but not verbally.

This extraordinary factor was what made it possible for major elements of the primary *Han* [Chinese] culture to spread to the far reaches of the huge country. But the language diversity continued to divide the people into cultural enclaves that made the western regions of the country more difficult to rule.

Shortly after Mao Zedong and the Communist Party took over China in 1949 he took the extraordinary

KEY WORDS CONTROL YOUR LIFE!

but commonsense step of decreeing that Mandarin, the language of the Beijing area of China, was to be the national language of the country, and mandated that it be taught in all elementary schools in the country. Now, most Chinese whose native tongue is not Mandarin are verbally bilingual.

The impact that the Chinese language has on the mind of the Chinese is far deeper and far more comprehensive than the influence of other languages on other people because the influence is both verbal and written.

All people who are not weaned on Chinese ideograms naturally react to both the sound and the written form of words in their own languages. But the reaction to words that are written with phonetic script is not nearly as strong as the reaction to pictorial ideograms that are representations of real things and explicit concepts.

Both the verbal and written forms of the Chinese language are therefore like massive software programs. They create and control the Chinese mind to a degree that goes well beyond the power of other languages.

This is the primary reasons why expatriate Chinese who have been out of China for several generations but have persevered in learning how to read and write *Hanzi* and speak the language have been able to maintain their Chinese cultural identity.

Becoming verbally fluent in Chinese and learning how to read and write some two thousand or more *Hanzi*

KEY WORDS CONTROL YOUR LIFE!

is a major undertaking that requires intense study and practice for one to three years.

However, it is not necessary to become fully fluent in Chinese in order to gain a comprehensive understanding of Chinese culture. And many people who *do* become quite fluent in the language as far as speaking and understanding is concerned still do not have a total grasp of the culture.

That requires full knowledge of the meanings and nuances of several hundred key terms in the language—words that incorporate and reflect elements of the culture in the deepest sense—and is a separate challenge in itself.

These are the terms I refer to as "cultural code words" because they are pregnant with cultural meanings that go far beyond their one-dimensional surface meanings.

TEN KEY WORDS IN MANDARIN

All languages are reflections of the emotional, spiritual and intellectual character of the people who created them, and the older, more structured and more exclusive a society and its language, the more terms it has that are pregnant with cultural nuances that control the attitudes and behavior of the people.

Here are introductions to 10 Chinese terms that are especially important for anyone interested in China for any reason.

KEY WORDS CONTROL YOUR LIFE!

Guanxi (Gwahn-she) / Connections

From the dawn of China's ancient civilization the people were controlled by beliefs, customs and laws that limited their ability to make personal and individual decisions. Virtually every aspect of their lives was prescribed, or was set by precedent, down to where they lived, what they wore, the work they did, the education they received, who they married, and how they interacted with other people.

Over the long millennia of Chinese history this system along with the beliefs and behavior that supported it became the foundation of the Chinese mindset. There was a precise Chinese way of doing everything.

In such a society the old adage "It's not what you know it's who you know" becomes an axiom of life. Another truism in this kind of society is the fact that it is generally not your intelligence, knowledge, ambition or motivation that deter-mines you success in life. It is *guanxi* (gwahn-she), the personal connections you have and how clever you are at using them.

Guanxi is usually translated into English as "connections," but this English term does not do justice to the cultural implications and importance of the word in Chinese society. In my above mentioned book I explain the concept of *guanxi* by defining it as relationships that are based on mutual dependence.

There is, of course, a certain amount of mutual dependence in all societies but in the American mindset in particular it is generally secondary to a strong sense of individualism and independence. Our mantra is that we take personal responsibility for our actions and our success or failure. Seeking and depending upon connections is not built into our way of life.

That is not the case in China. The essence of Chinese culture, still today, is based on *guanxi*. The foreigner in China who attempts to get by without making and nurturing connections is almost always doomed to failure.

2) Hou Men (Hoe-uu Mane) / The Back Door

In a society in which personal connections play a paramount role in all relationships—business, personal, political and otherwise—the typical Western way of doing things is often ineffective, and may be considered both arrogant and rude.

In China where historically ordinary people had no inalienable rights to protect them from those in power and where bureaucracy was universal and honed to perfection, expecting something simply because it was "right" and you should get it, and especially "demanding" something or some act-ion, would get the door slammed in your face, or far more serious results.

This situation resulted in the Chinese having to develop a variety of strategies and tactics to get things done—ways that were unofficial but were a key part of the system—like authorities allowing a black market to function because it provided them with advantages of one kind or another.

KEY WORDS CONTROL YOUR LIFE!

The most common of these unofficial tactics was using the *hou men* (hoe-uu mane) or "back door"—that is, contacting and making deals with people behind-the-scenes; in private.

Despite political reforms and cultural changes that have made life in China far more rational and practical, the use of *hou men* remains deeply embedded in the culture, and when there is a "back door" most people choose to take it—and if there isn't one they will generally attempt to make one.

This is usually one of the first lessons learned by foreigners working in China.

3) Bao (Bah-oh) / "Social Reciprocity"

In societies that do not have laws that allow people to deal with each other in an honest and fair way, relationships of all kinds—business, personal, political, etc.—must be based on trade-offs of one kind or another.

This means that people must first develop personal contacts and then all of the skills that are necessary to accomplish the results they want.

In China this cultural factor is known as *bao* (bah-oh), which may be translated as "social reciprocity." In my book on **China's Cultural Code Words** I also refer to it as "bartering social credits."

Despite the fact that the younger generations of Chinese, especially those with international educations, are gradually breaking away from the

KEY WORDS CONTROL YOUR LIFE!

restraints of *bao* in order to deal more effectively with foreigners, the use of "social credits" continues to play an important role in all aspects of life and work in China.

It is still advisable for foreigners assigned to China to build up *bao* with business contacts and government officials as rapidly and as widely as possible. Just as in the U.S. and elsewhere one of the primary ways of building up *bao* in China is hosting dinner and drinking parties.

People who are aware of the pitfalls of cross-cultural relationships do a lot of research before visiting the country in question.

4) Bi (Bee) / Unity the Chinese Way

The fact that many of the greatest feats of man-kind (building long canals, constructing great walls, creating thousands of full-sized terra cotta images of warriors to bury with a dead emperor, etc.) were first accomplished in China suggests that the Chinese long ago mastered the art of working together harmoniously and cooperatively.

But this image of China can be misleading to Westerners who are not familiar with the details of Chinese history or with the way the Chinese work together.

In reality the Chinese have always been independent-minded and individualistic but they have also always been under the iron fist of rulers who treated them like cattle, forcing them to behave and work in unison to survive.

KEY WORDS CONTROL YOUR LIFE!

Chinese philosophers preached about the wisdom of *bi* (bee) or "unity" and the rulers took their preaching to heart, but they used force to compel people to behave the way they wanted them to. And thus the **bi** of China was mostly a mirage.

Now that the heavy boot of the government is gradually being removed from the necks of the Chinese they are exercising varies degrees of freewill for the first time in their history, with the result that life in China has become more chaotic than ever before except in times of war.

Most Chinese are now out to get as rich as possible as quickly as possible, resulting in a lot of friction and frustration that alarms the government—and makes the lives of foreigners living and working in China a lot more unpredictable and interesting.

It is therefore important for foreigners in China to be aware of the historical role of Chinese style **bi**, and to use the term in its modern sense in their relationships with Chinese.

5) Budan Xin (Buu-dahn Sheen) / Chinese Style Sincerity

In China, as everywhere else in the world, people are very much concerned about sincerity in all of their relationships—because without it one's trust can be misplaced and abused with serious consequences.

But problems often occur in cross-cultural relationships despite the fact the both sides are aware

KEY WORDS CONTROL YOUR LIFE!

of the importance of sincerity and often harp on it in their presentations to each other.

Friction and frustration often occur between the parties for the simple reason that their cultural understanding of sincerity differs in a fundamental way.

The Chinese commonly use the term *budan xin* (buu-dahn sheen) in their references to sincerity and in their desire to have *budan xin* relationships with their foreign business contacts. This, of course, is always pleasing to the foreigners, and they readily agree that they too want sincerity with their business dealings.

These relationships are seldom without misunderstanding and friction, however, because in its Chinese context *budan xin* means "sincerity plus understanding"—and the catch is that this understanding means that *the foreigners are expected to understand the circumstance or position of the Chinese side, and accept it.*

This, of course, puts an entirely different slant on the concept of sincerity that prevails in the West, and it often happens that foreigners dealing with the Chinese must compromise their expectations and behavior to some degree if they want to do business with them.

As I have suggested elsewhere foreign business and diplomatic people who are newcomers to China would benefit enormously if they engaged the services of a bilingual bicultural Chinese advisor.

KEY WORDS CONTROL YOUR LIFE!

6) Buhe Luoji De (Buu-hay Loo-oh-jee Duh) / Fuzzy Logic

As I explain in my book **China's Cultural Code Words**, there are three kinds of logic in China: traditional, Communist and Western—and you have to know which one you are dealing with to understand what is going on.

Until the latter part of the 20th century Chinese in general were not allowed to behave in purely Western style logical ways, despite the fact that they could and did think logically in the Western sense in virtually all matters.

This situation is further complicated in present-day China by the fact that people who have been educated and trained to think and behave logically in Western terms will often behave in the traditional Chinese way by choice or in the Communist way because they have no choice.

The traditional Chinese way of thinking is what I call "fuzzy logic," meaning that it is not the hard two times two equals four kind of thinking or straight-line thinking. It is "holistic" thinking, or thinking in circles.

Since few Westerners are experienced in holistic or circular thinking, Chinese attitudes and behavior are often confusing to them. But fuzzy thinking (the term was actually invented by an American) is often far more powerful than "straight-line" thinking because it is takes in a lot more territory in terms of time, space and long-term results.

KEY WORDS CONTROL YOUR LIFE!

Westerners dealing with the Chinese should prepare themselves by learning how to use fuzzy logic.

7) Cheng (Chuung) / Personal Loyalty

Westerners are, of course, familiar with the concept of personal loyalty and are well aware of how important it can be in their lives. But their concept of the importance of personal loyalty pales when compared with that of the Chinese.

Again because the Chinese have never been able to depend upon their governments to detail and defend their rights with laws that applied to everyone, they have been on their own when it comes to avoiding problems, protecting them-selves and surviving in every sense of the word.

This situation has changed considerably in pre-sent-day China, but the average Chinese still has to depend upon the personal loyalty of family and friends to a far greater extent than Americans and other Westerners.

The Chinese therefore put great credence in developing and sustaining relationships that are based on strong *cheng* (chuung) ties. This requirement takes up a great deal of the time and energy of the Chinese when both of the parties involved are Chinese.

Interestingly enough, the Chinese can often develop strong *cheng* relationships with foreigners faster than they can with other Chinese because the cultural baggage that comes with Chinese relationships is far heavier.

KEY WORDS CONTROL YOUR LIFE!

Some Chinese and foreign relationships between businesspeople have survived time and war and become legendary.

The Chinese have very long cultural and racial memories—much longer than that of Americans—and it is important to keep that in mind.

8) Falu (Fah-luu) / Virtue vs. the Law

One of my favorite Confucian quotes (repeated in **China's Cultural Code Words**) is as follows:

"Attempting to rule people by laws that require them to act the same leads to resentment and disobedience of the laws, and to feel no shame!"

Confucius believed that people should behave because of their inherent virtue; not because of man-made laws.

The Imperial rulers of China (as well as the present-day Communist rulers to some extent) apparently took part of this philosophy to heart because most of China's *falu* (fah-luu) or "laws" were not codified or published. It was left up to judges and others to decide on what was legal and not legal.

In present-day China there are many published laws but many of them retain some of the essence of Confucius by being worded vaguely—so vaguely in many cases that their purpose cannot be clearly understood. [And when most people ignore them, the government sometimes pretends they don't exist; or that they were just a test.]

KEY WORDS CONTROL YOUR LIFE!

Like the emperors before them, China's Communist leaders know that if the laws are vague and punishments are quick and severe most people will refrain from doing anything that might even seem or arbitrarily judged to be illegal.

Still today the Communist government of China prefers to rule by directives rather than codified and published laws, which often puts foreign business people and others at a disadvantage because they cannot anticipate how the directives are going to be interpreted.

The only practical approach for foreigners is to get the advice and assistance of experienced Chinese—and hope for the best.

9) Hanyu (Hahn-yuu) / China's Secret Code

My referring to *Hanyu* (Hahn-yuu) as China's secret code is a bit of stretch that is intended to emphasize a key factor in China's historical and present-day relations with other people. *Hanyu* means "Chinese language" or "Chinese languages."

My point is that the existence of ten major Chinese languages (and dozens of minority languages and regional dialects) along with one of the most complex of all writing systems has traditionally served as the "Great Wall" of China—a wall that has helped keep the country isolated, insulated and exclusive until modern times.

KEY WORDS CONTROL YOUR LIFE!

In the past so few Westerners learned Chinese (mostly except for some missionaries!) that there was very little communication between ordinary Chinese and Westerners—and the bulk of that was with Chinese who had learned English or some other foreign language. As a result very few Westerners were ever able to fully understand Chinese culture.

This failing is gradually being remedied, as more and more non-Chinese are learning Mandarin (made the national language of China by the Communist Party in 1949)—and this includes Americans, who traditionally ignored language learning as an important skill.

But the "language wall" that has obscured China for so many millennia is far from being breached, and continues to present a challenge to the rest of the world.

One positive sigh: a growing number of American schools are offering lessons in Mandarin, the official Chinese language.

10) Gongwei (Goong-way-ee) / Flattery

To paraphrase an entry in my book, **China's Cultural Code Words**, there are many words in Chinese that are designed and used to show respect and deference to the elderly and superiors, to acknowledge social inferiority as well as demonstrate social superiority, to indicate sex and age differences, to account for extended-family relationships, to seek favors, etc. and etc.

KEY WORDS CONTROL YOUR LIFE!

This extensive vocabulary is a result of the vital importance that personal relationships have had in China since ancient times—which in turn resulted in people becoming extraordinarily sensitive to and about all of their relationships.

Another result of this situation was the role that *gongwei* (goong-way-ee), or "flattery," played in Chinese life.

With both success and survival generally de-pending on maintaining good relations with others—in the extreme sense—the use of flattery became a national custom that was raised to a fine art.

The use of *gonwei* is still deeply embedded in the character and personality of the Chinese, and has become one of their most valuable tools in dealing with foreigners. The Chinese learned a long time ago that Westerners—Americans in particular—are especially susceptible to flattery, and they use it with great skill to disarm and manipulate them.

Understanding and dealing with the Chinese goes well beyond communicating in general terms.

For a comprehensive explanation of 305 key Chinese words, see my book **China's Cultural Code Words**. Tuttle Publishing, the leading publisher on books about Asia based in Singapore and the U.S.
Available from Amazon.

KEY WORDS CONTROL YOUR LIFE!

THE JAPANESE LANGUAGE
The Vital Role of Japan's language
Ten of the Most Important Words in Japanese

In **Japan's Cultural Code Words** I noted that all languages are reflections of the emotional, spiritual and intellectual character of the people who created them. and that the older, more structured and more exclusive a society and its language, the more terms it has that are pregnant with cultural nuances that control the attitudes and behavior of the people.

In this respect key words in the Japanese language are doorways to understanding and dealing with the Japanese.

As said earlier one cannot understand or deal effectively with the Japanese in Japanese without knowing the most important key Japanese words.

Here are introductions to 10 Japanese terms that are especially important.

1) Wa (Wah) / Harmony

Wa (wah) expresses a Shinto concept of harmony between man, nature and all things in nature, and was what the Chinese called the Japanese islands long before the advent of Japan as a unified country.

In the 7th century A.D. Japan's reigning Imperial Regent issued a series of edicts that have since been referred to as the country's first "constitution." The

KEY WORDS CONTROL YOUR LIFE!

first of these proclamations was that *wa* was to be the foundation of Japanese society.

While *wa* has traditionally been translated into English as "harmony," it means much more than that in its Japanese context. In short, it means not doing anything that causes friction or upsets people or nature, and actively doing the things that ensure and sustain peaceful, cooperative, harmonious relation-ships.

In other words, *wa* means "Japanese style" harmony—not harmony in the Western English sense of the word.

During the 1960's and 70's when Japan's economic engine was running at full speed and was destined to make the small island nation the second largest economy in the world the Japanese incessantly attributed their amazing growth to the existence of *wa* in business, in government, in the educational system, and society in general.

All of Japan's traditional arts and crafts, etiquette, formal speech, cultural practices, etc. are infused with the essence of wa—of Japanese style harmony. As fellow writer Robert Whiting so eloquently noted in his book *You Gotta Have Wa!*, even the way the Japanese first played the game of baseball was also based on maintaining *wa* among all of the players on both teams—which often meant such things as taking the best players out of a game to avoid embarrassing the other team with high scores.

Still today to function effectively in Japan, foreigners must learn how to deal with the Japanese concept and practice of *wa*. The concept of *wa* is known in the

KEY WORDS CONTROL YOUR LIFE!

U.S. but it is generally not practiced in the full Japanese sense.

2) Amae (Ah-my) / Indulgent Love

Very early in the history of the Japanese the concept of *amae* (ah-my), which I describe in my book *Japan's Cultural Code Words* as "indulgent love," became a primary principle in the culture and one of the foundation of all relationships.

Its full meaning in a culture sense refers to being able to take advantage of other people in a co-operative spirit with the unstated commitment that they can do the same to you when the need arises.

The principle of *amae*, which no doubt derived from Shinto, takes precedence over egoistic feelings and the natural human instinct of selfishness, and is designed to ensure that society will function smoothly and efficiently.

Of course, this is an idealized concept of the desired attitudes and behavior of human beings—and one that has been a key aspect of many religions and philosophies—but in Japan where it meshed perfectly with the precepts of Buddhism and Confucianism, it actually became an integral part of the Japanese culture.

Both the word *amae* and the concept it refers to are still very much a part of the cultural make-up of the Japanese, and still plays a primary role in virtually all relationships—particularly so in business and politics.

KEY WORDS CONTROL YOUR LIFE!

You might say *amae* is a much stronger and more important element than the Western concept of "I will scratch your back if you will scratch mine." What it does in Japan is give the Japanese a great deal more leeway in how they handle their relationships with business partners and political allies.

They can, for example "break" some of the provisions of an agreement or contract when it is expedient to do so without unduly upsetting the other party because the other party has the "right" to do the same thing when it benefits them.

Learning how to use and accept *amae* behavior is not only a valuable asset in dealing with the Japanese there are numerous occasions when it is impossible to develop and maintain effective relations without it.

3) Kata (Kah-tah) / Form/Process

Many foreigners are familiar with the Japanese term *kata* (kah-tah) from its use in the martial arts where it describes the forms or processes used in training. But *kata* is far more important to under-standing and dealing with the Japanese than this implies.

The whole of Japan's traditional culture, from personal etiquette to how one learned to do all of the routine things in life, was based on *shikata* [she-kah-tah], the extension of *kata*—which means "way of doing things." The interjection of personal preference or deviation for any reason from the prescribed **shikata** was taboo.

There was a way of eating (tabe-kata), a way of reading (yomi-kata), a way of writing (kaki-kata), and

KEY WORDS CONTROL YOUR LIFE!

way of walking (aruki-kata), a way of talking (hanashi-kata), a way of doing things (yari-kata), and so on across the entire spectrum of Japanese behavior.

This prescribed and enforced conformity to exact ways of doing things had a profound influence on the character and personality of the Japanese—making them homogenous to an extraordinary degree as well as predictable because everybody was taught and trained to do things the same way.

It was also responsible for the remarkable manual skills that have long been typical of the Japanese, for their ability to focus on things with great intensity, and their compulsion to "get things right."

Still today no one can fully understand and appreciate the typical attitudes and behavior of the Japanese without knowledge of the *shikata* that made them.

For an early description of the influence of *kata* on Japanese behavior and how to deal with them, see my book, **KATA—The Key to Under-standing & Dealing with the Japanese**, published in 1990 and available from Amazon.

In 2014 I published an updated version of the kata factor in Japanese culture entitled *THE KATA FACTOR! – Japan's Secret Weapon!,* noting that the *shikata* [she-kah-tah] or "way of doing things" were gradually losing their influence among younger generations who are being programmed in the American way of thinking and doing things. It is available from Amazon.

KEY WORDS CONTROL YOUR LIFE!

4) Aisatsu (Aye-sot-sue) / Formal Greetings

Japan's traditional etiquette was one of the most structured, refined and sophisticated patterns of behavior ever imposed on any people. From infancy, the Japanese were trained physically and taught verbally how to behave in the prescribed manner.

There was no question about whether or not the young would be trained in etiquette or how they would be trained to behave. It was in integral part of the lifestyle—of being Japanese. Not behaving in the prescribed manner was a serious fault that could get one ostracized, if not eliminated.

The rules and forms involved in *aisatsu* (aye-sot-sue) or "greetings" were especially important between inferiors and superiors. The higher the rank of an individual, the more detailed the pre-scribed manner of greeting him or her, and the more rigorous the behavior was enforced.

The first Westerners to show up in Japan noted that the behavior of the typical Japanese was the kind one might expect of royalty.

Most young Japanese are no longer trained from infancy in the traditional behavior, but they con-tinue to absorb it from the culture and from witnessing it among adults as they grow up, and most of the traditional forms of etiquette are still followed by adults, particularly in formal situations.

KEY WORDS CONTROL YOUR LIFE!

The Westerner who really wants to "fit in" in Japan must learn a number of the more important forms of *aisatsu*, such as the formal greetings that take place in the business world during New Year's and on numerous other auspicious occasions, from weddings to funerals.

For a detailed description of Japanese etiquette, see my book, **ETIQUETTE GUIDE TO JAPAN---Know the Rules that Make the Difference**, Tuttle Publishing, available from Amazon.

---

5) San (Sahn) / Mr./Mrs./Miss

This simple little word is one of the most important terms in the vocabulary of the Japanese, and using it correctly is also one of the easiest things that foreigners in Japan can do—language-wise that is.

This version of *San* (Sahn) is the Japanese equivalent of Mr., Mrs. and Miss, and follows either the first name or the family name. In other words, Tanaka San may be Mr. Tanaka, Mrs. Tanaka or Miss Tanaka.

The attachment of *San* to family names has become so integrated into Japanese culture that is more like a part of the name than an honorific or term of respect.

Adults who have known each other from child-hood attach the *San* to each others' names when addressing each other in formal situations except when

KEY WORDS CONTROL YOUR LIFE!

they are out drinking together and get a little "high"—at which time they are culturally permitted to "dispense with etiquette" and use only first or last names.

In addition to people in general, *San* is also commonly attached to the first names of family members and close friends, especially when girls and young women are being addressed. Even mothers are inclined to attach *San* to first names when they address their children, especially when they are irritated by them or angry with them.

San also morphs into *Chan* (Chahn) when one is addressing younger family members and close friends by their first names. Yoshiko becomes Yoshiko Chan (Yoh-she-koh Chahn).

It is also customary to use *Chan* instead of *San* when using the diminutive of first names—but again this is only among families and close friends, and is generally limited to females.

The diminutive of Mariko is Mari—a common female name—which becomes Mari Chan. This is the equivalent of calling Robert "Bobby."

The point is, if you do not use Mr. Mrs. or Miss when addressing Japanese it is good manners to use *San*—and might be regarded as rude if you do not.

Addressing a young girl as *Chan* is very intimate, however, and should not be done by men unless they are close friends, the girls are very young, and the situation is informal. Of course, the more Westernized the girls are the less important this protocol.

KEY WORDS CONTROL YOUR LIFE!

6) O'kyaku san (Oh-k'yahk San) / Guest / Customer

The Japanese have long been famous for their attention to detail and the quality of their service to customers. This is especially true in the hospitality industries (hotels, inns, restaurants), in the entertainment industries (cabarets, clubs, inns that call in geisha, etc.), and in all forms of the retail business.

The reason for this level of attention and service goes back to the days of the shoguns, when the custom of royal service demanded by the shoguns, their ministers, feudal domain lords and samurai warriors eventually resulted in common people expecting and dispensing the same level of service in their own lives.

A key factor in the spread of refined service among the common people was that for over 200 years (1630s to 1867) the feudal lords of Japan were required to spend every other year in Edo (Tokyo), the Shogun capital, to serve at the Shogun's Court. This meant that they had to travel to and from their domains, with large retinues of attendants and warriors, stopping over nightly at inns along the way.

The feudal lords, like the shoguns whose behavior and expectations they imitated, required the highest possible level of service from the employees of the thousands of inns that dotted the country, resulting in the custom of service reaching levels in Japan that was unknown in other countries.

The essence of the level of service that is common in Japan's business world is reflected in the word

KEY WORDS CONTROL YOUR LIFE!

O'kyaku San (Oh-k'yahk San), the primary meaning of which is "guest."

In other words, customers are not just customers. They are "guests," with all of the cultural nuances this entails in behavior-conscious Japan.

7) Giri (Ghee-ree) / Obligations

Confucianism was introduced into Japan early in the history of the country, and was to have a profound influence on Japanese culture. Among the most important tenants of Confucian philosophy were the *giri* (ghee-ree) or obligations that children owe their parents, the young owe their elders, students owe to their teachers, and that all people owe to their superiors.

These obligations were natural and inherent. Broadly speaking, you were born with them as a result of your automatic relationship with your parents, elders, teachers, bosses, "lords" and so on.

As the generations passed these principles were enforced by a number of powerful social, eco-nomic and political sanctions, resulting in them becoming so deeply embedded in the culture that they were never questioned.

Interestingly, the most powerful of these sanctions was shame. Over time the Japanese became so sensitive about being shamed that avoiding shame became an overriding principle in their behavior; so powerful that many of them chose death—and often the death of their families—over shame.

KEY WORDS CONTROL YOUR LIFE!

The power of this feeling has been diminishing since the end of World War II in 1945 and the subsequent Occupation of Japan by American armed forces—a phenomenon that resulted in the partial Americanization of the younger generations

The ancient set of obligations that Confucius prescribed for people have also diminished dramatically in modern-day Japan, but they have not yet disappeared and are readily discernible in many situations, both social and professional.

Foreigners dealing with the Japanese on any level must be cautious about putting them in a position where they feel shamed—and remember that there have traditionally been two sides to being shamed. One was to commit suicide (which is now out), and the other side was to get revenge.

The Japanese are exceptionally skilled at getting revenge against people who have shamed them, generally sometime in the future to make the revenge sweeter.

(8) Tatemae/Honne (Tah-tay-my/Hoan-nay) / Façades and the Real Thing

The essence of Japan's traditional culture, which made being shamed one of the most terrible things that could befall a person, made a highly refined and structured etiquette mandatory and did not accept failure, resulted in the Japanese being extremely cautious in what they said and how they said it, especially when communicating with superiors and people with whom they had no binding ties or did not know.

KEY WORDS CONTROL YOUR LIFE!

This resulted in it becoming a deeply engrained habit for them to hedge their bets (so to speak) when communicating with others, meaning that they typically did not come right out and say what they thought in discussions that were more than just informal conversations.

In considering things presented to them and in negotiations it became customary to first present a *tatemae* (tah-tay-my), a facade or false front, first to protect themselves from any negative reaction, and second as a ploy to draw the other person out.

After a suitable period of both sides sounding each other out with facades, the next step was to present their *honne* (hone-nay), meaning their real thoughts; their real intentions.

The Japanese discovered a long time ago that Americans and Europeans generally present their real intentions first (lay their cards on the table), giving the Japanese an advantage in negotiating with them.

The tatemae and honne custom is still alive and well in Japan.

(9) Kao (Kah-oh) / Face

The Japanese are exceptionally sensitive to in-sults or slights of any kind, including things that Americans and many others ignore or laugh off. In such matters of protecting our name, reputation, etc., we have very thick skins while older Japanese often seem to have no protective skin at all.

KEY WORDS CONTROL YOUR LIFE!

This cultural element apparently derived from the fact that until modern times (post 1945) the Japanese were generally not allowed to express their individualism, their own preferences, except in ways that were traditionally sanctioned by their society—meaning doing only things their society approved of, and only then when they were done in the accepted Japanese way.

This meant that one of the few meaningful things that the Japanese had going for them was their *kao* (kah-oh), their "face," their reputation.

Losing face for the Japanese was therefore a very serious situation. When their face was trod on (so to speak), they were not only officially or formally allowed to complain they could in many situations, get even—including officially sanctioned attempts to kill the offenders.

Kao and *haji* (hah-jee), shame, were thus inextricably intertwined in Japanese culture, and still today play a significant role in Japanese life.

Foreigners dealing with the Japanese, for what-ever purpose, should keep this cultural factor in mind. When it is impossible to avoid saying or doing something that is very likely to smudge the face of a person, you can mitigate its effects by apologizing in advance. [Accepting responsibility and apologizing has great weight in Japanese culture.]

The Japanese typically apologize in advance when making speeches – a practice that some Americans have adopted. When an American says something

KEY WORDS CONTROL YOUR LIFE!

like "I'm going to insult you, so I apologize in advance," it gets a laugh.

10) Enryo (En-rio) / Holding Back

Any foreign lecturer or speaker who has ever given a presentation in Japan has almost always encountered the custom of older Japanese to *enryo* (en-rio), meaning "to hold back, "to say nothing," until they get the gist of the speech and approve of it.

The practice of *enryo* has been a characteristic of the Japanese since early in their history be-cause calling attention to themselves, speaking up, etc., was traditionally a very dangerous thing to do—and a trait that until very recent times the Japanese paraded as one of their primary virtues.

Of course, this is the opposite of the Western practice, and is therefore one of those areas where cross-cultural exchanges are sometimes disappointing to both sides—to the Japanese because from their viewpoint Westerners talk too much, and from the Western viewpoint because the Japanese don't speak up.

Before the turn of the century there was a great debate in Japan about the disadvantages they faced in their foreign affairs because they did not speak up clearly or often enough, and since the turn of the century leaders in many fields have been preaching a new mantra, saying that the Japanese must learn to speak up or continue to be taking advantage of in their relations with Western countries.

KEY WORDS CONTROL YOUR LIFE!

But there is often an advantage to Japanese negotiators when they sit quietly and wait.

The foreign negotiators, in an attempt to show goodwill and set an example, invariably reveal their position up front as fast as they can, unintentionally giving the Japanese an edge.

For more than 500 other extraordinarily insightful words in the Japanese language see my book **Japan's Cultural Code Words,** available from Amazon. **The Japanese Have a Word for It** and **Speak Japanese Today!** are also available from Amazon.

TEN KEY WORDS IN THE KOREAN LANGUAGE

In my book **Korea's Business & Cultural Code Words,** as in my other books on languages, I noted that all languages are reflections of the emotional, spiritual and intellectual character of the people who created them., and that the older, more structured and more exclusive a society and its language, the more terms it has that are pregnant with cultural nuances that control the attitudes and behavior of the people.

As the world knows, South Korea is a tiny nation on the southern half of the Korean Peninsula that has

KEY WORDS CONTROL YOUR LIFE!

one of the larger economies in the world, with huge industrial conglomerates that sell their high-tech products worldwide.

How this remarkable story came about—how this tiny nation of Asians that not too long age was part of a Hermit Kingdom that the industrial revolution had not touched—is not well known.

There are two things that help explain the amazing success of the South Koreans. One of these is that following the end of World War II in 1945 the southern portion of the peninsula came under the control of the United States, and despite a lot of stupid mishaps made it possible for the people of South Korea to develop a market and profit-driven economy.

The second factor that play a fundamental role in the incredible rise of South Korea is subsumed in the word *han* (hahn), which Korean scholars translate as "unrequited resentments"—which has to be explained because it means so much more than that phrase suggests.

My own definition is that *han* refers to all of the ambitions, all of the emotions, all of the desires, all of the natural impulses, all of the spirit, all of the intellectual impulses, that were oppressed and denied by the previous governments of Korea throughout the history of the country.

When all of these repressed feelings were released by South Koreans being freed from the oppression and restraints of the past, the energy and power and passion they were able to bring to their efforts to

KEY WORDS CONTROL YOUR LIFE!

create a modern economy have to have been seen to be fully appreciated.

This pent-up energy and passion of South Ko-reans has not yet expended itself, and going there and seeing the ferocity, dedication and diligence with which the people work is an astounding experience. The term *han* is not used in Korean speech.

North Koreans, on the other hand, are still beaten down and mired in the mud of the past by their misguided Communist overlords. They have not yet been freed from the chains of *han* and are now further restricted in their dealings with the outside world by a regime that makes a mockery of the natural insight and intelligence of humans.

1) Hanguk (Hahn-guuk) / The Korean Nation

The last line in the Korean national anthem does more to explain the pride and passion that South Koreans have in their nation than anything else I can think of. It goes like this:

"Let us love, come grief, come gladness, this, our beloved land!"

But to fully appreciate the passion and pride that all Koreans have traditionally had in their land you have to be a Korean—you have to know its history; its glories, its tragedies…especially its tragedies.

Over the past two and half millennia the Koreans have been invaded and occupied by the Chinese, the Mongols and the Japanese, and when they were not fighting outsiders they were savaged by internal

KEY WORDS CONTROL YOUR LIFE!

regional conflicts—and yet, despite these travails, Korea culture produced some of the world's greatest works of art, created masterpieces of poetry and made technical advances (including movable type for printing!) far earlier than any other people.

Another reason for the pride Koreans take in their nation is the natural beauty of the peninsula. The native religion of the Koreans, like that of the Japanese and American Indians, included the belief that they were a part of nature, and that recognizing and respecting the beauty of nature was a key part of their being.

Knowing the way Koreans feel about their *Hanguk*, and fully respecting their feelings, can be a major asset for foreigners visiting and living in Korea.

This is a type of behavior that causes many Americans problems because they have been conditioned to express their criticisms openly.

2) Enuri (Eh-nuu-ree) / Bargaining as a Social Skill

Foreign visitors who go shopping in South Korea and foreigners who engage in business with South Koreans should be aware of the traditions of bargaining in the country. Like all old societies, bargaining in Korea has traditionally been an important economic skill—and also like most people Koreans looked upon bargaining as a social skill as well.

Of course the reason for the early development and widespread use of bargaining is that until recent times there were no widely established principles for

KEY WORDS CONTROL YOUR LIFE!

setting the cost of goods or the value of labor. It was a matter of choice and need.

In today's Korea department stores, fine boutiques and the like have fixed prices, but in the great city markets, *enuri* (eh-nuu-ree), or haggling, to use a colloquial term, is still practiced by merchants and shoppers.

There is something else visitors should know about bargaining—and negotiating—in Korea. The typical Korean is a mastering at bargaining because the nature of their class and rank-based society has made it imperative that they develop verbal skills to a high level, and that they become especially clever at using emotional tactics in their bargaining.

This latter ploy is something that typically throws Western businesspeople for a loop because they have little or no experience in using emotion as a bargaining tool.

Koreans typically turn the negotiation of simple points into high drama by introducing various kinds of emotional elements. When this happens, the thing to do is to remain calm and collected and stick to your guns until your Korean counterparts accept the idea that you are not going to be bamboozled into anything.

3) Anshim (Ahn-sheem) / Peace of Mind Korean Style

It may be a bit difficult to accept the idea that Koreans have a deeply embedded need and desire for *anshim* (ahn-sheem) or peace of mind after you have

KEY WORDS CONTROL YOUR LIFE!

engaged in a bargaining session or had a personal encounter with someone. Koreans regularly engaged in loud arguments and verbal fights that can be upsetting to those who don't know what is going on.

But the influence of Buddhism and Confucianism had a powerful impact on the mindset of Koreans, programming them to be at ease and comfortable only in settings that are highly structured in which all of the traditional forms of etiquette are followed precisely. Of course, the younger the Koreans the less controlled they are by these ancient concepts.

Obviously this conditioning did not preclude loud verbal bouts and even physical action when they were done within the accepted guidelines.

In today's Korea the concept and importance of *anshim* continues to play a leading role. Korean culture continues to support the ideal of doing nothing to disturb the peace of mind of other people, in the use of language, in their personal relations, in the ethics they follow in business, and so on.

The main thing for foreigners to keep in mind is that *anshim* in Korea does not mean the same thing as peace of mind in the Western world. Some of the demands and dictates in Korea's business world, for example, go against everything Westerners hold dear.

Knowing when and how to develop and maintain *anshim* in Korea is an interesting challenge that requires substantial knowledge of the culture. Business people especially should take this to heart.

KEY WORDS CONTROL YOUR LIFE!

4] Chae-myun (Chay-me-yuun) / Saving Face

Because of the importance of social class and rank in pre-modern Korea all Koreans became incredibly sensitive about the behavior of others and their own behavior because there were so many things that could get them into trouble, and because there were precise forms of behavior that one had to know and follow to stay right with everybody.

This powerful cultural factor gave birth to *chae-myun* (chay-me-yuun) or "face-saving" as one of the most important, and demanding, aspects of Korean behavior. And in pre-modern Korea doing something that made someone else "lose face" or for yourself to lose face was not a trivial thing. It could be, and often was, disastrous.

Still today *chae-myum* continues to be a major factor in all relationships, particularly in work environments and in all professional categories. The way Koreans go about saving face often does not conform to Western concepts of what is necessary, right or acceptable—a situation that often causes friction between foreigners and Koreans working in the same company or organization.

In fact, some of the solutions Koreans choose are so far out from what would be a Western approach that they result in an impasse if not a complete breakdown in the relationship.

Here again, the only choice that foreigners in business situations have is to find out what the proposed Korean solution is before it is implemented

KEY WORDS CONTROL YOUR LIFE!

(they sometimes do it without informing the foreign side), and try to work out a compromise if they do not agree with it.

5) Changpi (Chahng-pee) / Shame

Like the Japanese, the primary sanction in maintaining and enforcing proper cultural behavior among Koreans was *changpi* (chahng-pee) or shame, which was generally self-imposed.

Instead of being programmed by a religion to feel guilty as a result of wrong doing, and being subject to punishment by the keepers of this religion-based method of control, Koreans were conditioned to feel intense shame, which turned out to be a more powerful control mechanism than guilt, resulting in Koreans (and Japanese) being far better behaved than their religious-oriented foreign counterparts.

Koreans still live in a shame-controlled culture—which is weaker than what it used to be but by Western standards is still incredibly strong. When Koreans themselves misbehave in any way, the feelings of shame are powerful.

When they are shamed by someone else's behavior toward them, the sense of shame is generally even more powerful, and invariably calls for some kind of revenge.

The role of shame in Korean culture derives from the influence of Confucianism, which teaches that personal shame should be the basis of all morality—not religious or secular laws.

KEY WORDS CONTROL YOUR LIFE!

In earlier times, one of the major sources of shame for male Koreans was failing to live up to the expectations of their families, their fathers, their close kin and their clan. Now it is more likely failure to live up to their personal ambitions.

Here, also, it is important for foreigners dealing with Koreans to know enough about the culture to be aware of the kind of things that result in shame—and both avoid them and learn how to deal with them if they happen inadvertently.

Again, for executives of foreign business firms who are newcomers in Korea it is very important for them to retain the services of a bilingual, bicultural Korean as an advisor.

Failing to do this invariably results in the ruffling of Korean feathers..

6) Chib (Cheeb) / The Korean Family

There is a lot of talk in the United States and other Western countries about the importance of family, but the Western concept of family and the role the family plays in Western cultures pales in comparison to the family in Korea.

To understand and appreciate the importance and power of the family in Korea one must fully understand the Korean term *chib* (cheeb), which literally means "household."

The essence and role of the *chib* in Korean society goes back to the teachings of Confucius, which holds

KEY WORDS CONTROL YOUR LIFE!

that respecting and obeying parents is one of the primary principles of morality.

For millennia Korea was known as the most Confucian-oriented country in Asia and this was reflected in every facet of Korean culture, but especially in the family where the father ruled supreme and women and children could not make decisions or act on their own.

One could say that in the Western sense individuals did not exist in traditional Korean society. Children were taught and required to think and behave in terms of their *chib* to avoid bringing any kind of dishonor to their family, to protect the family, to ensure its continuity.

The family was in reality the building blocks of Korea's hierarchical social and political order that was based on absolute submission of inferiors to superiors.

While the role and importance of the family in Korea has weakened significantly since the mid-20th century it is still a major factor in the lives of the people—again far more important than in most other countries.

Among other things, adult Koreans will almost always consult with their families in order to get their approval before making decisions about work and other such matters. They almost never act on their own.

Foreign companies operating in Korea must keep this factor in mind in their management policies and

KEY WORDS CONTROL YOUR LIFE!

practices. One of the things that smarter foreigner business people do is retain bilingual, bicultural Koreans as advisors.

7) Chingu (Cheen-guu) / Cultivating Friends

Friendships are obviously important in virtually all societies, for business as well as social reasons, but few people go as far as Koreans in their compulsion to develop and keep *chingu* [cheen-guu], or friends.

The reason for this extraordinary behavior is that traditionally Koreans could not depend upon anyone except people with whom they had close personal and family ties…basically for anything, often including services that local officials and bureaucrats were obliged to do for them.

The obligations that family members had to each other and to their family as a whole virtually precluded them from establishing close relationships with more than a few outsiders. Most women spent their lives without ever speaking to, much less spending time with, anyone not a member of their family or close kin.

For one long period in the recent history of Korea women in urban areas could not leave their family compound during the day to shop or pay social visits. They were allowed to leave the compounds for a few hours only at night, during which men were required to stay indoors in order to keep the two sexes segregated.

KEY WORDS CONTROL YOUR LIFE!

Men had a lot more freedom than women, but their outside relationship were generally limited to contacts made in bars and *kisaeng* (kee-sang) Korean geisha houses. They were not free to develop a circle of friends in the casual way that is common in Western countries.

These strict political controls ended near the end of the 1800s, but it was to be several decades before both men and women in Korea felt free to exercise the kind of personal freedoms Americans and others take for granted.

However, the legacy of the past is still very much alive in present-day Korea when it comes to friends and friendships.

Koreans, especially men, go out of their way to develop and maintain a circle of friends because it is invariably through friends that they are able to get things done…a custom that foreigners in Korea need to be aware of and follow.

8) Chinshim (Cheen-sheem) / The Vital Role of Sincerity

When Koreans meet outsiders (meaning non-Koreans) their cultural antenna is always up and turned on. Their antenna is set to read many things about the people they meet—and one of the most important of these things is subsumed in the word *chinshim* (cheen-sheem), which translates as "sincerity."

KEY WORDS CONTROL YOUR LIFE!

And not surprisingly, *chinshim* in its Korean context means a lot more than sincerity does in its English context. The reason for this difference is that for millennia in Korea there were no laws that protected the people or guaranteed any personal rights.

None of the many things that Westerners (now at least) can take for granted in their relationships with other people existed in pre-modern Korea—except with family members and the few personal friends that Koreans were permitted to have.

One of the very first things that Koreans at-tempted to measure in new people they met was their degree of *chinshim* (sincerity), and in its Korean context *chinshim* refers to a wide range of things—philosophical, spiritual and ethical as well as general character—which had to be of a high order to be acceptable, much less impressive.

Like all of the traditional cultural attributes of Koreans their concern with *chinshim* has decreased since the mid-1900s, but it remains an important part of their character and plays a significant role in their lives.

Among other things, when companies interview potential new employees there are a number of things that are on the top of their list—their name (which tells an enormous about the history of their family), what region of the country they were born in (also historically meaningful), where they went to school, and the level of their *chinshim*.

Foreign employers who ignore these factors are almost always disappointed by their new hires becaused the new people want and expect these

KEY WORDS CONTROL YOUR LIFE!

factors to be a key part of the getting acquainted process. When they are not the new employees never feel fully comfortable.

.9) Chiwi (Chee-wee) / Rank Has its Privileges

In strict hierarchical societies such as Korea rank is of vital importance because it is one of the primary foundations of such societies—you must know or quickly learn the *chiwi* [chee-wee] or rank of everyone you meet and have anything to do with because rank de-termines your language and your behavior toward others, how they treat you, and what you can, and may, get from them.

Until well into the 20th century Korean society was one of the most hierarchical-ridden societies in the world. People belonged to specific classes and categories within classes that were structured on an inferior-superior basis with very precise and very strict rules controlling behavior.

This factor made Koreans among the most rank-conscious people on the planet and although considerable diminished from pre-modern days rank-consciousness is still an important facet of Korean culture.

In larger Korean companies, for example, the atmosphere can be very much like that at a strict military academy, with rigid formality between the ranks of the employees and managers and very little (if any) of the joking and casual chatting that one encounters in typical American companies.

KEY WORDS CONTROL YOUR LIFE!

This separation by *chiwi* also generally follows that of strict military organizations when it comes to longevity in a company. Employees who joined a company last year, for example, regard themselves as outranking those who joined this year, even though they may officially be on the same level in the company.

It behooves foreign companies setting up operations in Korea to be acutely aware of the importance of rank to Koreans in their management policies and practices—and this includes social as well as educational "rank."

10) Chok (Choak) /
Clans are Alive and Well in Korea

Koreans trace their history back to just a few family clans that entered the peninsula from the north or northwest. Over the millennia these clans grew, and although they eventually populated the entire Korean peninsula, they remained intact and fiercely protective of their identities and names.

Very early in the history of Korea leadership of the *chok* (choak) or clans became hereditary, with the families of the leaders becoming the royal houses and therefore vitally concerned about their genealogy.

From those earliest times down to the 20th century Korea's society remained distinguished by its clans, with only a few families controlling the country—which was often divided into different regions under the control of one clan or another.

KEY WORDS CONTROL YOUR LIFE!

Although these ancient clans have survived into modern times and the original families still make up most of the elite of the country, democracy, individualism and a highly industrialized economy now overshadow their influence. But they are still important in matters of marriage, employment and political success.

Foreigners dealing with Korea would be wise to make themselves aware of the clan relationships of their Korean contacts, and to diplomatically sound them out about their family histories.

Of course, when younger generations of Koreans are concerned the influence of these age-old customs has diminished considerable, especially among the younger ones who have learned to speak English.

For a comprehensive analysis of the character and personality of Koreans (and of course we are talking about South Koreans) based on 213 key words, see my books **Korea's Business and Cultural Code Words**, and **Korean Business Etiquette,** both available from Amazon. Tuttle Publishing.

KEY WORDS CONTROL YOUR LIFE!

ASPECTS OF THE JAPANESE MINDSET & BEHAVIOR

COMMUNICATING IN JAPANESE!

One of my books, **JAPAN! – A New Way of Getting the Most Out of a Japan Experience,** gets down to the nitty-gritty on: (1) the frame of mind you need to have for a rewarding visit—or stay—in Japan; (2) on what you should know before you get there; (3) on the effect seasons will have on your visit; (4) on the background of Japan's cultural attractions; and (5) on off-beat things that regular tourist itineraries do not cover.

These insights and information add a special dimension to the Japan experience even if it is just for a few days. The book also includes Japanese language vocabulary and common everyday expressions that will add a fourth dimension to your visit.

All of these words and expressions are rendered in Romanized letters and in English phonetics that duplicate their Japanese pronunciation, meaning that when you speak or read the phonetics out loud the sounds come out "in Japanese!" Here are some examples:

Good Morning / Ohayo-gozaimasu
[Oh-hah-yoe-go-zie-mahss]

KEY WORDS CONTROL YOUR LIFE!

Used from early morning until about 10am when you are meeting or calling on an individual for the first time that morning.

Hello / Good day, Good afternoon / Kon-nichi wa [Kone-nee-chee wah]

Used from about 10am until dusk or just before.

Good Evening / Komban wa [Kome-bahn wah]

Used from the onset of dusk until midnight.

What is your name? /

Onamae wa nan desu ka?
[Oh-nah-my wah nahn dess kah?]

How are you? / Genki desu ka?

I'm fine / Genki desu [Gane-kee dess]

Being able to say a number of key things in Japanese will totally change the flavor of your visit. You can easily memorize the simpler greetings and expressions in advance.

For a full home-course in Japanese, see **SPEAK JAPANESE TODAY - A Little Language Goes a Long Way!,** available from Amazon.

With the number of Japanese traveling abroad for business and pleasure being able to say just a few words to tourists and business people will totally change the flavor of the encounter.

KEY WORDS CONTROL YOUR LIFE!

HIGH-TECH SENSE OF THE JAPANESE
Catching Up With Star Trek!

Japanese scientists continue to make advances in technology that could—and probably will—provide people with the opportunity to change the very nature of the way they live in ways that are both exhilarating and frightening.

The closest analogy that one can use to visualize what has already happened and is continuing to happen in Japan's research institutes is the kind of technology that science fiction writers have been visualizing for more than a century, and have been epitomized in recent decades by such television fare and films as *Star Trek*.

For those who are not *Star Trek* fans the series of TV shows and films began with a proposal in 1961 by writer/director Gene Roddenberry for a science fiction series that was set some three hundred years in the future when space travel and traveling far faster than the speed of light were routine; virtually all diseases had been conquered, people no longer had to work to produce things, and money no longer existed.

One of the more astounding abilities of computers in that far-off future was the creation of virtual worlds that were as real to the five senses as anything in the real world. The virtual worlds created by these futuristic computers were used for both research and entertainment.

KEY WORDS CONTROL YOUR LIFE!

Whatever scenario the future computers were programmed for they could instantly create in a seemingly limitless space called a holodeck...and as far as the people who entered the holodeck were concerned the situations they experienced were real to all of their senses—including [not surprisingly] some sexy scenes.

In the real world, in real time, Japanese scientists have been working on the creation of such *Star Trek*-type virtual scenarios for several years and have continued to make dramatic steps forward. Such progress is almost always exponential—the more progress you make the more likely you will make more. [The *Star Trek* series went on to become one of the most influential and profitable franchises in film history.]

In addition to making progress in creating virtual worlds that are real to the five senses, Japanese scientists are adapting variations of the tech-nology to a number of other mind-boggling uses.

These present-day practical uses include turning digital devices on-and-off with the mind without wires attached to the head; a guidance system that does not use a visual screen or map-like readout to direct drivers and pedestrians to locations they are not familiar with; produce 3-D images that are mergers of past and present events and in effect recreate history and allow people to not only view 3-D images of things like valuable art or museum pieces from different viewpoints but actually *touch* them.

One of the most fascinating things this new tech-nology will do is provide people with the means of

KEY WORDS CONTROL YOUR LIFE!

creating virtual versions of their lives to pass on to their children and grandchildren—not just one-dimensional photos and printed materials.

Also not surprisingly, among the first uses of this convergence of technology will be games for the young that are entertaining, and educational material that incorporates all of the senses in the learning process, including hands-on learning.

Two of the industries that are bound to pick up on this technology are the sex trade and the religious trade—a use that was envisioned by science fiction writers as far back as the 1940s.

GETTING OFF THE BEATEN TRACK!

Most people who visit Japan as tourists are kept on a pre-set course that takes them to and by a variety of attractions, limiting their experiences to a small sampling of the diversity and richness that make up the essence of life in Japan.

The depth and breadth of the whole of Japan experience is incredible and cannot be packaged into several days or even several weeks.

However, even visitors who are bound by time constraints and well-beaten tours can enliven and enrich their experiences by participating in at least a few unique customs and practices.

This ranges from visiting areas in Tokyo and elsewhere that have retained the look and flavor of Japan's feudal Shogun era, to spending time in one

KEY WORDS CONTROL YOUR LIFE!

or more of the remaining castles that were the homes and fortresses of fief clan lords from the 1600s to 1870.

AMAZING FACTS ABOUT JAPAN!

Japan is known worldwide for its economic prowess and such iconic symbols as geisha, karaoke, manga, Mt. Fuji, ninja, feudal-age samurai warriors and huge sumo wrestlers.

What is not so well-known are its amazing historical artifacts [shrines; temples; castles; the world's largest and oldest wooden buildings; arts and crafts, hundreds of annual festivals that go back nearly two thousand years]; the incredible scenic beauty of its mountains, gorges, rivers, one of the longest and most gorgeous coastlines in the world; and a combined modern and traditional lifestyle that is so fascinating and seductive that exposure to it for just a few days is a mind-altering experience.

My book, **AMAZING JAPAN – Why Japan is One of the World's Most Intriguing Countries!,** identifies and describes a choice selection of things that make Japan one of the world's most unusual, most intriguing, and most enjoyable travel destinations – things that explain why so many foreigners take up permanent residence there once they have experienced life in this amazing country.

One of the key elements in this attraction is the ritualized behavior of the Japanese that make them predictable and the best behaved people in the world.

KEY WORDS CONTROL YOUR LIFE!

Japan's Shogun Era Only a Doorway Away!

For really old Japan-hands who have been involved with the country since the late 1940s and early 1950s the cultural-social changes that have occurred are mind-boggling, and yet elements of the traditional culture that go back even before the last samurai-dominated Shogun dynasties [1603-1867] remain a significant part of the Japan experience.

All one has to do to step back hundreds of years of time in Japan is go through the door of any of thousands of inns, restaurants, shrines and tem-ples that provide the same ambiance, the same sense of serenity and aesthetics that were a hallmark of life in Japan for more than a thousand years.

The recent advent of the Internet, personal com-munication devices and the online social media have initiated new widespread changes in the way the Japanese think and behave, and even this has not replaced the essence of traditional Japan; the sights, sounds and tastes that have defined a unique culture for millennia.

Beginning in the mid-1950s its seemed inevitable that traditional Japan was doomed; that it could not withstand all of the changes taking place—changes that were greeted and welcomed by the younger generations who, in fact, felt compelled to "de-Japanize" themselves.

And then as the year 2000 approached a growing number of Japanese, young and old, began to

KEY WORDS CONTROL YOUR LIFE!

reconnect with the values and lifestyle of the past. They began to realize that something of infinite value had been lost and they began rediscovering the sensual, intellectual and spiritual pleasures that had made life in pre-modern Japan so satisfying.

This trend continues today, but that does not mean the end of new things and new ways developing in Japan that have their own cachet; their own appeal. And as un-Japanese as it first sounds, one of these new things that has already become institutionalized in the mass culture is American style outdoor barbecues.

Interestingly, the royal families of ancient Japan were the first to institutionalize outdoor picnics.

Eating outdoors at food stalls, both stationary and mobile, is in fact very old in Japan; going back to the earliest days of the country.

In the 1950s food carts still lined the main streets of major shopping and entertainment districts and mobile food carts prowled neighborhood streets, their owners calling out the specialty they served. You still find food carts in and near parks, temples and other public places.

Among the newest and biggest things are barbecues organized and staged in dedicated areas by public barbecue catering companies in sizes that range from the relative small and intimate [15 to 20 people] to those that attract well over a thousand guests.

The foods served at the catered barbecues range from traditional favorites to American and European dishes—some of which require large ovens. Special dishes are available for kids. During the cold winter months and the rainy seasons the catering services set up tents on the outside barbecue grounds. A number of transportation companies, including Fujikyuko, that have covered facilities have gotten into the business.

Barbecues that are open the public offer another way for the Japanese to come together to socialize with strangers—something that they did not do in the past. The barbecues also offer resident foreigners and visitors an opportunity to mingle with groups of Japanese in situations that have their own distinctive ambiance.

My advice for Westerners visiting Japan is to bypass modern Japan and go back in time to the days of the samurai and shoguns. In fact, several sections of Tokyo have turned back the clock of time, resurrecting the glory days of Edo culture. Just ask your hotel concierge to point the way.

There is—or at least was the last time I was there—a floor of the Haneda International Airport in Tokyo that has a Shogun era floor with authentic shops and restaurants.

VISITORS CAN LEARN ABOUT JAPAN'S AMAZING NINJA!

One of Japan's most successful exports is the image and lore of the *ninja* [neen-jah], a special breed of

KEY WORDS CONTROL YOUR LIFE!

secret agents who began playing an extraordinary role in the political life and strife of Japan around the 14th century—with antecedents that go back another 600 years.

The mysterious nature of the *ninja* has long captured popular imagination in Japan and made its way into Western cultures in video games and films.

Ninja figure prominently in folklore and legend, and as a result it is often difficult to separate historical fact from myth. Some legendary abilities attributed to the *ninja* include invisibility, walking on water, and control over natural elements—all things the *ninja* could actually do with special techniques and equipment.

In the 15th century during a long period of civil wars between contending provincial lords the demand for secret agents became large, resulting in whole clans in the Iga and Koga regions of Japan becoming "ninja clans," with both male and female members of the clans trained in all of the arts and skills of assassination, espionage and spying, using special techniques and devices invented and perfected for all of the challenges presented by these activities.

The role and number of *ninja* decreased drama-tically following the unification of the country under the powerful Tokugawa Shogunate in 1603, but during the Tokugawa era [1603-1868] a series of books about the exploits of the *ninja*, both fact and fiction, were published and became bestsellers.

In the 1950s Japan's movie industry picked up on the *ninja* theme. In the 1960s the image and lore of the

KEY WORDS CONTROL YOUR LIFE!

ninja began to spread to the outside world via movies, TV shows and cartoon books, with a number of foreign actors [and a few actresses] becoming major stars in *ninja* roles.

This led to millions of kids around the country becoming *ninja* fans.

What most visitors to Japan may not know is that the world of the *ninja* has been recreated in the city of Iga in Mie Prefecture in the mountains that separate Kyoto and Nagoya, and is one of the most fascinating attractions in the country.

Large numbers of tourists—who apparently got hooked on *ninja* lore when young—now visit Iga to watch authentic performances by *ninja* actors using the tools and techniques that made real *ninja* such formidable assassins and spies, and whose real exploits, as noted, make James Bond look like a namby-pamby boy scout.

The Iga style of *ninjutsu* [neen-jute-sue], translated as "the art of invisibility," was the most developed, the most sophisticated and the most sought after by the clan lords during the long civil wars of the 14th and 15th century, and the city of Iga now makes the most of it.

In addition to an *Iga-ryu [style] Ninja Museum* on the grounds of Iga's Ueno Castle, where *ninja* performances are staged, there is also a *Ninja Tradition Hall*, where visitors can learn about the history of the **ninja** and a *Ninja Experience Plaza* where visitors can watch demonstrations.

KEY WORDS CONTROL YOUR LIFE!

The busiest period at "Ninja Town" is April and May, especially during Japan's famous Golden Week, an extended vacation period during which the Iga Ueno Tourist Association sponsors a *n*inja festival.

During the festival visitors can experience using some of the *ninja's* most famous weapons, like the-*shuriken* [shuu-ree-kane]—a small wheel-shaped throwing device that could stop a target in his tracks or kill him if aimed at the head, and blow-darts that were equally effective in stopping a victim.

In October each year the museum hosts a *shuriken* competition, which attracts up to a hundred participants who must follow strict rules regarding the size, weight and material of the *shuriken*. Winners are typically awarded with special *shuriken* made of gold.

You don't have to be a *ninja* fan for a trip to Iga to add a special touch to a Japan visit. It is a place where history comes alive.

Japanese Girls Going After Geeks & Nerds!

The twists and turns of Japanese culture since the mid-1950s have ranged from exciting and uplifting to bizarre...even grotesque...and a new phenomenon fits several of these categories at the same time!

This new phenomenon evolved out of the term *otaku* [oh-tah-koo], which more or less means "your hon-

KEY WORDS CONTROL YOUR LIFE!

orable house" or "your honorable self" when talking politely and/or formally to someone.

Somehow, this term came to be applied to boys and young men who had become obsessed with the new *anime* [ah-nee-may] comics and *manga* [mahn-gah] cartoons that began to appear in Japan a few years after the end of World War II in 1945, and gradually grew into one of the publishing phenomena of the times.

For decades, however, the term *otaku* had a negative connotation since it referred to young males who were so obsessed with *anime* and *manga* that they ignored virtually everything else, from their appearance to their body odor, and had no life outside of their obsession…especially with girls. Being referred to as an "otaku" was, in fact, derogatory to the extreme.

The term *otaku* showed up in the U.S. in the mid-1980s, where it was used as a slang term for boys and young men who had also become *anime* and *manga* fans, but without the negative overtones. In fact, some of its American users began equating it with guru.

In Japan, on the other hand, the label continued to be very negative and became even more onerous in 1989 when a man accused and convicted of several murders became nationally known as "The Otaku Murderer."

But following the beginning of the 21st century something that is very common in Japan began to occur—an extraordinary cultural shift initiated and led by females.

KEY WORDS CONTROL YOUR LIFE!

Teenage girls and young single women had become frustrated by the fact that most ordinary Japanese males did not know how to interact well with females and did not make ideal boyfriends or husbands. They began to look more closely at the large tribe of *otaku* boys and young men in the country, and they liked what they saw.

They found that the typical *otaku* was intelligent, kind, caring and otherwise so unlike non-otaku males that they did not appear to be "Japanese." This discovery led teenage girls to begin forming relationships with *otaku*. Then older still single women began following their example.

Female fashion designers picked up on the new phenomenon. Clothing shops and other businesses in such famous teenage hangouts as the Harajuku district in Tokyo began catering to *otaku* couples. Organizations designed to bring *otaku* and young women together began proliferating throughout the country.

In the spring of 2012 a female author published a book that portrayed the present generation of *otaku* as studious and hard-working, especially supportive toward women, and having good commonsense when it came to pursuing professional careers and their personal interests—areas in which non-otaku males were notoriously weak.

This book put the seal of approval on the new "geeks are good for girls" phenomenon and fueled what the news media soon began referring to as a national movement of females chasing *otaku*... naturally adding to the ardor of girls and young women seeking to meet and mate with *otaku*.

KEY WORDS CONTROL YOUR LIFE!

The *otaku* movement goes well beyond its immediate influence on the lives of thousands of young Japanese males and females. It represents the beginning of a major shift in male-female relations in Japan...and is yet another example of how Japan's young girls and women have initiated and led virtually all of the fundamental changes in Japan's social culture since the end of the samurai/shogunate era in 1878.

In the meantime, many American girls still go for jocks instead of geeks...and live to regret it.

As it turns out, jocks are generally manly and look sexy to females but they are less likely than geeks to take the feelings of their female companions or mates into consideration.

Japan's Amazing High-Tech Factory-Farms

The great tsunami wave that inundated and destroyed a great swath of the coastline and inland farming areas of Fukushima Prefecture northeast of Tokyo in 2011 had a remarkable effect on the mindset and behavior of younger generations of Japanese.

Unlike their predecessors their reaction did not reflect the traditional regionalism that had historically divided the Japanese into exclusive cultural pockets ruled over by *daimyo* [die-m'yoh] or provincial fief lords. They behaved as family members do when disasters strike.

But this was not the only fall-out from the tsunami. Farmers whose crops and lands had been deva-

KEY WORDS CONTROL YOUR LIFE!

stated by the great wave made a giant leap forward in agriculture by adopting the new LED [light-emitting diodes] technology to provide the sun-light energy that plants need to grow.

Instead reclaiming and cultivating soil in the traditional way of growing vegetables and fruits they built "farms" inside of buildings that were totally independent of natural sunlight and the outside climate—an approach that was first introduced in 2004 by an entrepreneur named Shigeharu Yamamura, the founder of a small company called *Mirai* [Me-rye], which means "Future," but had been ignored by farmers as well as government entities.

The 2011 tsunami that rocked the nation [and moved the main island of Honshu several inches closer to the Asian mainland] provided the spark that Yamamura needed to get his revolutionary concept off and running.

By March 2012 there were 106 factory farms in the country with more being added regularly—"farms" that were completely independent of the problems presented by the location, the time of the year and the prevailing climate.

Mirai Inc. began leasing its " LED factory-farm" technology both domestically and internationally, and it has since been spreading around the world.

One of the Japanese companies that picked up on the LED-farming technology was textile manufacturer Nisshinbo Holdings, Inc., which has over 70,000 strawberry plants in just one of its factory-farms. The factory, in Tokushima, ships strawberries the year-around.

KEY WORDS CONTROL YOUR LIFE!

Farm-factories using the LED technology can alter the wave-length of the light emitted to change its color which signals plants when to germinate and when to flower and controls the quality of the taste.

Another element in the this new factory farm phenomenon is that the fertilizers used in the process—fed to the plants by the watering system—can be precisely controlled to get the desired combination of nutrients, fundamentally effecting the health benefits of the produce.

In 2012 Japan's huge trading conglomerate Marubeni Corp. formed a partnership with Mirai Inc. to sell its factory farming technology in China—something that will have an absolutely astounding effect not only on the food supply in China and the employment of millions of peasant farmers, but also on its exports.

Mirai Inc. also formed a joint-venture with agricultural interests in Mongolia and began exporting plant factory equipment to that country.

In 2013 Mirai Inc. began construction of the world's largest vegetable factory in Tagajo City in Miyagi Prefecture, north of Fukushima Prefecture where the tsunami hit. Built on 1,000 square meters of land, the factory was designed to produce 10,000 heads of lettuce a day everyday of the year—that's 3,600,000 heads per year!

As suggested in a previous column there is no way that traditional farming methods can compete with this new way of farming, and its impact on the world at large will be perhaps even more remarkable than the original development of farming some 10,000 years ago.

KEY WORDS CONTROL YOUR LIFE!

But given the astounding advances scientists are making in manipulating atoms to create new materials factory farming will probably not last for more than a hundred years at most.

By then, as in *Star Trek* [also previously noted] computer-controlled equipment will transform base materials into whatever people want to eat and drink...just as 3-D Printing has already begun to supplement the traditional product manufacturing process.

And the further along this high-tech development the less need there will be for ordinary manual laborers.

Saving the Sexy "Cover-It-All-Up" Kimono!

People who are not intimately familiar with Japan's traditional [female] kimono may never have thought of the "cover-everything-up" garments as particularly sexy, but they are. Even the most die-hard take-it-all-off advocates cannot deny their influence on both the girls and women who wear them and the libido of males who view them.

The first step in converting full or nearly full-exposure die-hards to an appreciation of the seductive appeal of kimono is to remind them that total exposure of the female body eventually results in a loss of its seductive powers...

In ancient times the Japanese learned that mystery and the imagination are far more powerful sexual

KEY WORDS CONTROL YOUR LIFE!

turn-on's than complete exposure of the body, and until recent times this knowledge was reflected in their wearing apparel as well as in other areas of their life, including communal bathing.

Furthermore, early Japanese, being especially sensually oriented because of their Shinto beliefs, did not leave the seductive powers of form-fitting kimono to just concealing rather than revealing the physical charms of girls and women. They added the power of colors and design elements to further enhance the sensual appeal of the garments.

But many of the lifestyle changes that were introduced into Japan from the 1870s on were incomepatible with the kimono, and over the next century it gradually disappeared from everyday wear.

By the 1970s one generally saw kimono only on special occasions such as weddings and holidays. It began to seem as if this amazing garment had been consigned to the dust heap of history.

And then in the early 1970s manufacturers began an attempt to revive the popularity of the kimono by producing cheaper versions of them in cotton and linen, rather than the traditional silk—itself one of the most sensual fabrics ever made. The enormous but latent cultural power of the kimono kicked in and in no time the industry was worth ¥2 trillion a year.

But the new cotton and linen kimono had a short lifetime, their cost continued to spiral upward, and sales began to decline. By 2007 sales were off by about 75 percent, resulting in something quite new for Japan: the appearance of low-cost kimono rental

KEY WORDS CONTROL YOUR LIFE!

services and large numbers of retailers specializing in secondhand kimono.

Now, a growing number of people, particularly middle-aged and older women and men, rent kimono for special occasions, including to wear while strolling around in traditional neighborhoods, to attend kabuki and noh performances, and to visit famous historical sites.

One traditionally styled restaurant in Tokyo's Kagurazaka district [the Shinari] rents kimono to patrons who make reservations in advance, allowing them to have a totally traditional dining experience.

Since many Japanese have never worn kimono before, rental services [and the Shinari restaurant] assist their patrons in putting the garments on properly. Rental fees for up to eight hours cost between $50 and $70 as of this writing.

As of this writing retail shops say their bestsellers to younger women are in the $300 to $500 range, while older women are inclined to buy more expensive versions. Some shops carry kimono made of denim as well as cotton and linen—the denim appealing more to men than to women.

Traditional silk kimono are still made in Kyoto for really wealthy clientele, and cost from $15,000-$30,000. If properly cared for these kimono can last for half a millennia or more and become family heirlooms, passed from generation to generation.

Renewed interest in wearing kimono is reflective of the latent power of Japan's traditional culture and a growing unease with the style of living and working that came with the modern economy.

The effect that a kimono has on teenage girls and young women in particular is remarkable—their attitude and behavior changes. They must walk in a more sedate manner that is conspicuously sensual. They *feel* the sensuality of the colorful, form-fitting garments, and it shows in their manner.

Both the change in the physical appearance and the behavior of young women in kimono have a subtle but powerful affect on the libido of males...which is certainly not lost on the females!

Interestingly, a growing number of foreign women are discovering the potency of kimono and adding it to their arsenal of feminine wiles.

Understanding the *Yugen* Element In the Beauty of Japanese Arts & Crafts

When Westerners first began to visit Japan in the mid-1500s they were struck by the refined beauty and quality of the country's arts and crafts. It was a kind of beauty and quality that they had never seen before.

This special quality of Japanese things was so commonplace that the Japanese themselves did not consider it unusual. Everything they made, including simple household utensils, had the same quality.

KEY WORDS CONTROL YOUR LIFE!

Japan's traditional arts and crafts owed their special character to a merging of cosmic and Shinto concepts of harmony, sensuality and spirituality—a cultural factor that remains very much in evidence and in force among Japanese artists and craftsmen in present-day Japan.

The Shinto concept of harmony included the size and shape of things, how they were to be used, and their relationship with people. The spiritual element in Japanese things incorporated the essence and spirit of the materials used, and was based on both respecting and revering these inherent qualities.

The sensual element in Japanese arts and crafts was reflected by the things that people automatically find attractive—harmony in shape, in size, in the relationship of the parts, in the interaction of colors, in their feel when touched, and in the vibrations they project.

After generations of refining their designs and techniques, Japan's master artists and craftsmen achieved a kind and quality of beauty that transcended the obvious surface manifestations of their materials—a kind of beauty that was described as *yugen* (yuu-gane), meaning "mystery" or "subtlety."

Quoting from my book *The Elements of Japanese Design*: "*Yugen* beauty refers to a type of attractiveness—beneath the surface of the material but in delicate harmony with it—that registers on the conscious as well as the subconscious of the viewer. It radiates a kind of spiritual essence."

The skill and techniques that were going into Japan's arts and crafts by the 10th century became so deeply

KEY WORDS CONTROL YOUR LIFE!

embedded in the culture that they were not distinguished from daily life, and were reflected in everything the Japanese did, from designing and building castles, gardens, homes and palaces to the creation of hand-made paper.

Despite the mostly Western façade that today's Japan presents to the world *yugen* [yuu-gain]beauty is still very much in evidence in the arts and crafts, in traditional restaurants, inns, shops, wearing apparel and else-where in many unexpected places.

Yugen is another Japanese word I recommend that other people learn and use because it clearly identifies a concept that in other languages requires several sentences to explain — and in itself is an example of the traditional Japanese propensity to refine things down to their essence.

This compulsive reduction tendency of the Japanese is also dramatically demonstrated in their ability to design and manufacture miniaturized hi-tech products and in using nanotechnology to create new processes and new materials.

For a definitive look at the Japanese view and creation of *yugen* beauty, see *Elements of Japanese Design—Key Terms for Understanding & Using Japan's Classic Wabi-Sabi-Shibui Concepts*, available from Amazon.

KEY WORDS CONTROL YOUR LIFE!

Innovations, Inventions Changing "Samurai" Lifestyle

The ongoing presence and purity of Japan's traditional culture in so many areas of life is one of the most amazing aspects of modern Japan, particularly so since from the early 1870s the Japanese as a whole adopted foreign lifestyles with a skill and speed that was astounding.

The primary reason for this susceptibility and virtual obsession with change was the fact that historically life in Japan was so structured, so homogenized, so intellectually limiting that people hungered for change for almost anything new.

In fact, from the mid-1600s until 1867/8 the reigning Shogun governments did their best to enforce a law that banned virtually all change. And again from the 1870s to the mid-1900s the new nationalistic government controlled the lives of the people to the point that generally they were still not free to innovate or invent on their own.

But all of this was to change dramatically following the introduction of personal freedom (democracy!) into Japan at the end of World War II in 1945. With their knowledge, ambitions and skills unleashed for the first time in the history of the country the Japanese began an incredible flow of inventions and innovations that have continued to transform their lives—not to mention the lives of millions of people around the world.

KEY WORDS CONTROL YOUR LIFE!

These changes were so "un-Japanese-like" that most Westerners who were intimately familiar with all areas of Japanese history simply could not see or accept them. [In 1954 the dean of foreign correspondents in Tokyo told me that I should go home because Japan would "never amount to anything!" and there was no future in staying there!]

In fact, it was not until the early 1970s, by which time Japan had technologically and productively passed the United States in many areas, that Westerners in general and Americans in particular began to realize that Japan was on the verge of economically colonizing the world.

This resulted in hundreds of thousands of American and European business leaders flocking to Japan to learn why and how the Japanese had succeeded in transforming their tiny country into an economic superpower.

Large numbers of these visitors whose businesses were in peril went with their hands out, seeking loans and investments to salvage their mismanaged companies.

Many American companies did not survive, and it took some ten years for the survivors to learn and implement the production techniques and management practices that had catapulted Japan into the forefront of so many industries, and finally begin to turning their own companies around.

The Japanese continue to be world leaders in scientific and technological advances that are having fundamental affects on virtually every field of human

KEY WORDS CONTROL YOUR LIFE!

endeavor. There are so many basic breakthroughs that Japan-watchers have a hard time keeping up with them.

Some of the new things introduced in recent weeks and months will result in major business and lifestyle changes. One that immediately comes to mind is technology developed by apparel maker Konaka Company for producing fabric for suits that makes it possible for them to be washed at home in a shower instead of being sent to dry cleaners.

Following the Japanese penchant for catchy and unusual brand names these new suits are known as "Shower Clean Suits." Detergents do not have to be used to get the suits clean and ironing is not necessary if they are dried in the shade.

Not surprisingly, the "shower suits" are selling like the proverbial hotcakes, resulting in dry cleaning businesses having to increase their prices to remain profitable – which is boosting the sales of the shower suits and putting more pressure on dry cleaning establishments to continue raising their prices…!

This new technology will undoubtedly spread to most if not all other kinds of wearing apparel that now requires dry cleaning, obviously threatening the existence of dry cleaners in general.

Another break-through product that could have a far wider impact is the development of a paint that reflects light and keeps painted surfaces from 15 to 30 degrees cooler than those painted with regular paint, including white paint.

KEY WORDS CONTROL YOUR LIFE!

This new paint technology, developed by the Tokyo firm Nagashima Special Paint Co., and called Miracool, works with any color of paint, including black, which means it has widespread use on build-ings, sidewalks, blacktop highways, etc. The paint is sold by Miracool Co., a subsidiary of the developer.

Another recent fascinating Japanese development: a pillow with a built-in sound system that calms, soothes and otherwise "mothers" newborn babies. The developer: advanced medical equipment maker TLS Co., in Takaoka, Toyama Prefecture.

New Elements Adding To the Ambiance of Life in Japan!

-A new phenomenon in Japan based on enjoying dark nights prompts memories of a time in the late 1950s and early 1960s when residents of Tokyo and other cities were not able to see the stars at night because of thick clouds of pollution that totally obscured the skies.

Children who had never been in the countryside at night, away from the cities with the worst pollution, had never seen the moon or the other wonders of the night sky.

But Japan's pollution problem had been mostly resolved by the mid-1960s, and now both residents and visitors alike could enjoy an element of life that recalled the days of preindustrial Japan, when moon-viewing, star-gazing and the ambiance of city lights at night – viewed from the hills within and surrounding

KEY WORDS CONTROL YOUR LIFE!

the cities -- were an important part of the ambiance of Japanese culture.

Entrepreneurs operating restaurants and other businesses located in high-rise buildings in the major cities have modernized this ancient custom by providing onsite "view concierges" to point out to patrons interesting places within the cities that can be seen at night.

These nighttime sightseeing services are being used by people in general, particular out-of-town visitors, as well as young men looking for especially romantic date places and memorable spots for proposing marriage.

Tourism companies have also begun adding some of these high-rise view spots to their nighttime itineraries – recalling the time in early Japan when there were dozens of nationally famous view-spots around the country that attracted thousands of travelers annually, all of whom traversed the country's network of great roads on foot...on cultural and recreational journeys that could last for months.

Today these same spots attract hundreds of thousands of visitors annually – with one of my favorites being Matsushima Bay, about 40 train minutes from Sendai, north of Tokyo.

Matsushima means "Pine Islands," and refers to the hundreds of pine tree-clad islets in the bay— presenting a sight that is sublime in its beauty. It is one of Japan's famous "Scenic Trio" of sights so compelling they cannot be adequately described– the other two being Amanohashidate on the Japan Sea

KEY WORDS CONTROL YOUR LIFE!

coast north of Kyoto, and Itsuku Island in Hiroshima Bay.

In keeping with the Japanese penchant for formalizing and institutionalizing things, the new "view concierges" are certified as trained "view navigators" who have attended seminars on the history of their areas, color psychology [!] and other topics, and have passed examinations.

These nocturnal tour guides include taxi drivers, employees of hotels and others who have a special interesting in knowing more about their cities and providing a unique service to residents and visitors.

One restaurant in Yokohama [Next Yokohama Bay] has become so popular because of its spectacular nighttime views of the bay that all of its seats were normally reserved from weeks to months in advance.

Another even more dramatic element in nighttime touring was that offered by airships over Tokyo, Osaka and other cities. These tours, which generally lasted for about an hour and a half, could cost over a thousand dollars, but that was not an obstacle to their success.

Unlike helicopter tours, the cabins of airships were located some distance away from their engines, significantly reducing the noise and providing a much more comfortable atmosphere for passengers.

Visitors who do not have the time -- or money -- to book airship tours or patronize restaurants with view concierges had only to visit any of hundreds of high-rise office and other buildings in Japan that have whole floors devoted to restaurants with view windows. Many also have observation decks that provide extraordinary views night and day.

In Tokyo the Roppongi Hills Mori Tower in the famous Roppongi entertainment district has one of the best observation decks. It is on the 52nd floor and is circular, so you can walk around it and get a 360-degree view of Tokyo, including Tokyo Bay, Odaiba Island, Rainbow Bridge, the Imperial Palace Grounds, the clusters of high-rises in the city's major business, hotel and shopping districts, and Mt. Fuji some 60 miles away.

Secrets of Japan's Appeal to Westerners

When the first Westerners of record stumbled onto Japan in the 1540s, the discovery of the islands resulted in an influx of foreign traders and Christian missionaries, mostly from Macau, both aimed at- expanding their empires in Asia.

Among the many things that astounded these first European visitors to Japan was the incredible quality of its handicrafts and arts and the ability of Japanese craftsmen to copy any Western product not only perfectly but to improve on it in the process.

European traders who took up residence in Japan from the mid-1500s on began to ship large quantities of Japan's arts and crafts to the capitals of Europe, where many of them became collectors' items. Europeans found their aesthetic appeal both se-

KEY WORDS CONTROL YOUR LIFE!

ductive and fascinating, and still today that appeal is one of the secrets of Japan's attraction to visitors from around the world.

What was the source of Japan's traditional quality standards? How were the Japanese able to raise the quality standards of their handicrafts to that of a fine art? This too, relates to their skill in copying and improving upon things they copy, but in this case it goes back well over a thousand years.

Beginning around 300 A.D. Chinese ideas and products began trickling into Japan, mostly through Korea and via Korean immigrants to the islands. Along with these products came the ancient Chinese custom of the master-apprentice approach to the arts and crafts.

But the Japanese didn't just imitate the Chinese and Koreans. They institutionalized and ritualized the master-apprentice training methods, adding to it the concept of *kaizen* (kigh-zen) or continuous improvement. Within a few generations these products produced by had been totally Japanized and their quality raised to the level of fine arts.

As the generations passed, these institutions and rituals were further strengthened by the introduction of the Zen principles of dispensing with the superfluous and harmonizing life and nature, resulting in masters who could actually achieve virtual perfection in the arts and crafts.

This was the Japan that Westerners first encountered in the 1500s and again in the 1800s, by which time, the Japanese were so conditioned in the principles

KEY WORDS CONTROL YOUR LIFE!

and practices of quality that they didn't have to think about it. Achieving it was simply the Japanese way of doing things.

Another important factor that continues to distinguish Japan's traditional arts and crafts, as well as many of its modern products, is a look and a feel that is unique, that grows out of the psychic of the Japanese that precedes their contact with Korea and China—something that was programmed into their culture by Shinto, their native religion, which holds that all things have spirits and a beauty of their own and that it is up to craftsmen to bring both of them out.

The influence of this "Japanese thing" on Westerners varies from very weak to very strong, depending on their sensitivity and aesthetic development. But it influences everyone to some degree. To the sensitive person, it has a calming, soothing effect on the intellect and the spirit, and creates a harmonious repose with nature.

Americans and Europeans who visit Japan, even for a few days, are invariably touched by this unique facet of Japanese culture.

Visitors to Japan do not have to go out of their way to experience this extraordinary influence of Japan's arts and crafts—and to take some of it home with them if they choose.

Examples of Japanese arts and crafts can be seen in shops, in Japanese style restaurants, in traditional inns and in hotel arcades. Every department store in the country carries a range of the very same arts and crafts that so impressed the first European visitors more than 400 years ago.

Japanese Scientists Copying Nature!

In 1971 the American academic journal *SCIENCE* published an article reporting the existence of anti-freeze proteins in the blood of fish that thrive in the Antarctic in water that is so cold it would freeze other life forms in a matter of seconds or minutes.

SCIENCE later reported the discovery of the same antifreeze proteins in wild oats, winter rye, other plants and bacteria. This was followed by reports announcing that similar proteins had been found in frogs and insects.

As has often happened, however, it was Japanese scientists who began major research programs to turn these discoveries into new industries that would change the quality of many of the frozen foods consumed by people.

In simple terms, the anti-freeze proteins injected into foods prior to freezing significantly reduces the degree to which small water crystals in the items are transformed into large crystals—a phenomenon that dramatically changes their taste when they are thawed out for consumption, making them spongy and mushy.

By limiting the size of the water crystals to their normal size the antifreeze proteins result in the food items retaining their texture and flavor—a boon to

KEY WORDS CONTROL YOUR LIFE!

food manufacturers and consumers alike...and proof once again that nature provides life forms with the ability to survive and thrive in the environment they originated in no matter how extreme.

In the U.S. these discoveries led to the mass-production of antifreeze proteins as an additive for ice-cream, but the Japanese were to go much further.

Public and private laboratories in Japan began introducing antifreeze proteins into a wide variety of food items, including eggs, meats, noodles, pizza dough, rice and sashimi [raw fish]...and food manufacturers rushed to take advantage of the new technology.

Much of this advance followed the discovery and development in 2008 by scientist Osamu Shimomura of a green fluorescent protein derived from jellyfish that could be used to tag other proteins that might have useful applications—a discovery that won him the Nobel Prize in chemistry.

As is often the case with new break-through discoveries Shimomura was not looking for a green fluorescent protein when he first began examining jellyfish. He was trying to find out what made them light up.

Kaneka Corporation's Frontier Biochemical and Medical Research Laboratories have been leaders in identifying anti-freeze proteins in different life forms and applying them to different foods destined to be frozen.

Kaneka's research labs also began working in co-operation with Kansai University Prof. Hidehira Kawa-

KEY WORDS CONTROL YOUR LIFE!

hara to identify and study antifreeze proteins in different plants and organic life forms.

They discovered that antifreeze proteins in plants are not there to keep them from freezing but to keep them from drying out. The proteins trap the water molecules in the plants.

Japan's National Institute of Industrial Science and Technology was the leader in developing the technology necessary to isolate and purify antifreeze proteins from fish for industrial use.

The number of applications for antifreeze proteins has since expanded rapidly...something that future astronauts and others who depend on frozen foods will no doubt appreciate.

And as a side note: scientists have also confirmed that human beings also develop new genes to cope with the environment they live in...an obvious sign that nature does not distinguish between humans, ants frogs, rats, weeds, or any other life form!

In humans these environmentally induced genes affect skin color, the color of the hair, the size and shape of the eyes, the color of the eyes, the ability to withstand cold and heat, and other mental and physical attributes. In other words, human beings are made by their environment—just like all life forms.

KEY WORDS CONTROL YOUR LIFE!

Places to Go to if You Think You Have "Seen" Japan

There are several dozen UNESCO World Heritage Sites in Japan that provide authentic views of the unique culture that has made Japan fascinating not only to the Japanese but to visitors as well for over a thousand years.

One of these places is a village community named Shirakawa-Go in the township of Hida in Gifu Prefecture. Situated in mountains that are snow-covered during the winter months, the village attracts some 1.3 million visitors a year.

The village is famous for its ancient Japanese style buildings but its biggest draw is an equally ancient process of drying strips of cloth colored with natural dyes on beds of snow under the brilliant sunshine.

The dyes are made from local plants and fruits. The long strips of cloth are dyed by teams of women who flap them high into the air to catch the warm rays of the sun. The timing of the drying process is a crucial mattering in getting the colors desired because the dyes act differently at different times, depending on how the sun hits them.

Shirakawa-Go is about three bus/car hours from Nagoya Station. The trip from Osaka Station also via highway takes about four hours, and from Tokyo it is about five-and-a-half to six hours.

Travel agencies offer packaged tours to the remote picturesque village, and that is the best way to make the journey since it eliminates any problems involved

KEY WORDS CONTROL YOUR LIFE!

in getting there and back. It can add a remarkable element to a Japan trip that often begins and ends with big cities.

THE EXOTIC ORIENT

The exotic side of the Orient has always fascinated both Western men and women who were fortunate enough to visit there. But it has been the erotic side of Oriental life that has resulted in large numbers of Western men, beginning with Marco Polo, spending years or the rest of their lives in the Far East.

I deal with key aspects of Japan in several of my books, including:

AMAZING JAPAN! Why Japan is One of the World's Most Intriguing Countries

EXOTIC JAPAN! The Sensual & Visual Plea-sures!

THE BIZARRE & THE WONDROUS FROM THE LAND OF THE RISING SUN

JAPAN Aspects of a Unique Culture that Attracts Foreigners

MISTRESS-KEEPING IN JAPAN! The Pitfalls & the Pleasures

WHY THE JAPANESE ARE A SUPERIOR PEOPLE!

THE KATA FACTOR! Japan's Secret Weapon!

KEY WORDS CONTROL YOUR LIFE!

A Remarkable People-Future-Oriented Enterprise

Japan's Taisei Corporation, a major construction company with offices in all of the country's major cities as well as overseas, is noted for adhering to a strict principle of building people-friendly community-oriented projects and "green buildings" that make use of the latest technology for heating and cooling and for leaving the smallest possible footprint on the environment.

Taisei is especially noted for its "building for the future" policy rather than simply to make a profit, which is the motive of most construction companies.

A principal aspect of this policy is Taisei's building structures that protect against natural disasters such as earthquakes and tsunami [tidal waves].

One of the latest examples of this is a so-called "Evacuation Shelter" that looks something like an old-fashioned farm silo with a wrap-around enclosed stairway to the entrance at the top of the structure.

The shelter is a cylindrical building made of reinforced concrete that is several stories high and is designed to protect people from tidal waves such as the one that devastated the Fukushima coastal areas northeast of Tokyo in March 2011.

The round tower is surrounded by pillars at 2-meter intervals that are designed to break up tidal waves and reduce their impact on the structure. A spokesperson for Taisei said the structure could withstand waves that were 8 meters [24 ft] high.

KEY WORDS CONTROL YOUR LIFE!

The Evacuation Shelter will hold up to 150 people and enough food, water and other supplies to last them for several days as they wait to be rescued.

Taisei has proposed that regional municipalities in areas that are subject to earthquakes and tsunamis engage it to build a number of the evacuation shelters in key locations. It has also suggested that private companies with factories and other facilities in dangerous areas along the coast should also consider making the shelters a part of their infrastructure.

The estimated cost of one of Taisei's "Evacuation Shelters" was said to be about ¥300 million. Taisei engineers add that the shelter offers 30 percent more protection from killer tidal waves than ordinary reinforced buildings.

Given the natural disasters that have struck areas of the United States and other countries in recent years it would seem that such shelters would be a wise investment for many overseas communities.

Getting Taken for a Ride In Japan!

In the late 1800s and early 1900a visitors to Japan, Hong Kong and China invariably came across the famous rickshaws that served as taxis. Rickshaw is "short" for *jinriksha* (jin-rick-shaw), which itself is a shortened form of the original Japanese phrase *jinrikisha* (jin-ree-kee-shah), which translates as "human-powered-vehicle."

Oddly enough, it seems that the first rickshaw-type human-powered vehicles appeared in Paris in the

KEY WORDS CONTROL YOUR LIFE!

1600s—not in Asia—and were adaptations of wheel barrows used to transport vinegar around the city—thus the French name vinaigrettes for these early "taxis."

As far as Asia is concerned, Japanese sources say that the jinrikisha was invented by three Japanese men, Yosuke Izumi, Tokujiro Suzuki and Kosuke Takayama in 1868 as an adaptation of the horse-drawn carriages that had been introduced from the U.S. a few years earlier.

In 1870 Japan's newly installed Meiji government issued an exclusive permit to these three men to build and sell rickshaws to the general public. The seal of these men were required on every license to operate a rickshaw.

According to the rickshaw museum some 40,000 rickshaws were operating in Tokyo by 1872, and for the next several decades they were the chief form of public transportation in Japan. They were especially popular among the thousands of geisha and well-to-do patrons of the courtesan districts.

Interestingly, the first rickshaws in Hong Kong were imported from Japan—not mainland China—in 1874, and were a popular form of transport there for many years, peaking at more than 3,000 in the 1920s.

During the last decades of the 19th century rickshaws also appeared in many other Southeast Asian cities—and pulling a rickshaw was often the first job for peasants migrating to these cities.

In Hong Kong today one sees only a few rickshaws, mainly concentrated at the ferry landings in Kowloon and on Hong Kong Island for use by tourists.

KEY WORDS CONTROL YOUR LIFE!

Back in Japan, most jinrikisha were replaced by cars in the 1930s, but during World War II and in the years immediately following the war they made a brief comeback because of the scarcity of automobiles and gas.

However, rickshaws have remained the preferred form of transportation for many geisha, and traditionally styled rickshaws can still be seen in the geisha districts of Tokyo and Kyoto.

But there is now something new in the way of rickshaws on the streets of Tokyo and a growing number of other cities. In 2002 Japanese entrepreneurs began importing a modernized version of rickshaws called velotaxis from Germany, where they first appeared in the early 1990s.

The three-wheeled German-made velotaxis sport a space-age lightweight plastic cab that is open on both sides, with a passenger seat behind the peddler - driver. They cater to tourists as well as residents who enjoy their ambiance when going sightseeing and shopping in central areas of the cities.

As with regular taxicabs, velotaxi fares are based on distance, but are about one-half to one-third of the cost of regular taxis. One velotaxi operator in the popular Sannomiya and Motomachi districts of central Kobe features sponsored ads on its velotaxis, and does not charge passengers.

Most of the velotaxi companies also offer their cabs for political campaigns and other events held by cities and companies—a use that is said to be growing from 20 to 30 percent a year.

KEY WORDS CONTROL YOUR LIFE!

The velotaxis travel at about 10 kilometers per hour (6mph). On main streets they are required to travel on the far sides of streets outside of the lanes used by regular traffic.

Visitors to Japan should consider adding the velotaxi experience to their agenda, both for the novelty of it and because they can often be more convenient and practical than regular cabs, especially in crowded shopping and entertainment districts.

Cultural Ways of Pleasuring In the Brevity of Life!

One of the most memorable afternoons I have spent in Japan was in a traditional *ryokan* (rio-kahn), or inn, situated on the slope of a gorge on picturesque Izu Peninsula southwest of Tokyo.

It was a Sunday afternoon. I was alone, and it was raining—not a heavy rain but a light, steady rain that was close to being a mist. I was sitting on the balcony of my room, looking out over the gorge, waiting for a friend to arrive.

As I sat there I began to experience what the Japanese call *mono no aware* (moe-no no ah-wah-ray)—a Buddhist concept that includes being very conscious of the ephemeral nature of man, his struggle in the face of great odds and the inevitability of his downfall and disappearance.

This aspect of Japan's culture, developed between 700 and 1200 A.D. was based on the acute recognition of the impermanence of all things—an element

KEY WORDS CONTROL YOUR LIFE!

that later was enhanced by the code of the samurai which required them to be ready to give up their lives at a moment's notice—resulting in their lives being compared to cherry blossoms...beautiful but fragile to the extreme and subject to being wafted away by the slightest breeze.

This culture of impermanence was especially reflected in the haiku and tanka poetry of the era, as well as in the such great literary works as *Genji Monogatari* (The Tale of Genji), a novel about the intrigues and loves of an imperial prince (usually regarded as the world's first novel) written in the early 11th century by Murasaki Shikibu, a lady in the Imperial Court in Kyoto; and *Heike Monogatari* (The Tale of the Heike), compiled by a blind monk named Kakuichi in 1371.

The opening lines of Heike Monogatari, which depicts an epic struggle between the Taira and Minamoto clans for the control of Japan in the 12th century, say more about the human condition than many philosophical tomes:

"The sound of the Gion Shôja temple bells echoes the impermanence of all things; the color of the sâla flowers reveals the truth that the prosperous must decline. The proud do not endure, they are like a dream on a spring night; the mighty fall at last; they are as dust before the wind."

The culture of Japan reflected this theme in many ways, resulting in the Japanese developing an extensive vocabulary that expressed this inherent sadness of life.

KEY WORDS CONTROL YOUR LIFE!

While *mono no aware* means something like "indulging one's self in grief," neither this phrase nor any of the other key words were actually used in sad situations. Instead they referred to a gentle melancholy view of the fragility and preciousness of life that included an element of subdued pleasure.

The annual custom of celebrating the short life of cherry blossoms is the largest of Japan's the *mono no aware* rituals. It reminds them to take the time and find ways enjoy life while you can because it will soon be gone.

My spending a quiet afternoon entranced by the natural beauty of the setting as it was being cleansed and renewed by rain was another of the *mono no aware* practices that are dear to the hearts of the Japanese. Still another way is to engage in "forest bathing"—spending time in an isolated forest, letting the sights, sounds and vibrations of the trees wash over you.

There is also an element of *mono no aware* in most of Japan's classic art and craft designs, from kitchen utensils to the kimono wore by older men and women. The famous Tea Ceremony is a pure *mono no aware* ritual.

Knowledge of this cultural element makes it possible for one to appreciate more fully the distinctive essence of things Japanese—the elements that make them Japanese.

And this factor is one of the unspoken and generally un-described things that makes the traditional aspects of life in Japan so sensually, intellectually, and spiritually attractive to everyone, including foreigners

KEY WORDS CONTROL YOUR LIFE!

who are sensitive to the realities of life, including its brevity.

The Changes in Meeting & Mating in Japan!

Until Japan's long Shogun era ended in 1868 virtually all marriages were arranged by professional matchmakers, aunts, uncles, or bosses in the workplace.

Following the end of the Shogun era dating and courting among 20-somethings, followed by marriage, was more or less confined to upper-class young people whose families had become internationalized to some degree. Self-arranged love marriages among common people remained few and far between.

The introduction of democracy in Japan by the United States in the latter half of the 1940s still did not revolutionize meeting and mating in Japan.

From the mid-1950s on most young Japanese men became so busy—so obsessed with working long hours six and seven days a week—that they didn't have time to meet and court potential wives.

The traditional customs that had kept young men and [non-professional] women from intimate relationships prior to marriage remained a significant barrier. Most young Japanese men and women simply had no experience in meeting and dating members of the opposite sex.

For one thing, eligible young women did not go to bars, clubs, dances or parties as they do in the U.S.

KEY WORDS CONTROL YOUR LIFE!

and Europe. Bars and clubs, many stocked with female hostesses, catered exclusively to men.

These barriers eventually gave birth to large professional match-making enterprises that put marriage go-betweening on a business level. Then along came the Internet and new high-tech versions of match-making. And still meeting and mating on an individual personal basis remained inadequate to meet the demand.

To add to this, a growing number of female 20-somethings opted for a career rather than early marriage...pushing the average marriage age up to 27 or so. The number of unmarried men and women in their 30s ballooned.

And then another wrench was thrown into the mix, causing more problems. Companies began promoting and paying employees on the basis of merit, which resulted in bosses having to distance themselves from the employees under them instead of treating them like family and arranging marriages for them.

By 2005 the number of couples who met at their workplaces or were introduced by bosses and work colleagues plummeted to less than 30 percent.

All these factors combined resulted in the growth of online meet-and-match services where men and women could sign up and mine their data basis for likely partners. At first, most of the users were men, but then the number of female members began to grow—a phenomenon that gave birth to a new word *konkatsu* [kone-kot-sue], referring to the act of looking for potential marriage partners.

KEY WORDS CONTROL YOUR LIFE!

Konkatsu was made up of the parts of two common terms: *shukatsu* [shuu-kot-sue], meaning to seek employment at a specific company, and *kekkon* [keck-kone], meaning marriage.

The term *konkatsu* was first used on a popular TV show that depicted men and women ferreting out information about members of the opposite sex, and from there quickly spread across Japanese society—giving a name and an identity to a social problem that had become serious in the eyes of the government because the population had been falling for the past several years.

This has resulted in the government initiating a number of programs to encourage more Japanese men and women to meet and mate—something many other countries around the world need to do in reverse to reduce over-population.

Japan's New "Marriage Hunt" Phenomena!

Japan is having a serious problem with its population—a problem that is just the opposite of what most countries are experiencing. Several year ago the population of Japan began decreasing at a rate that alarmed the country to the point that dire predictions were commonplace and a number of drastic steps were introduced to encourage young men and women to meet and mate.

KEY WORDS CONTROL YOUR LIFE!

The falling population had an effect on virtually every facet of life in Japan, from educational facilities to the ability of companies to find enough employees to keep their production high and competitive with the rest of Asia.

The decreasing enrollment of students in public and private schools resulted in them suffering financially, which had an impact on their ability to hire and keep the best teaching talent. A growing number of Japanese corporations began moving their production to other countries, not only because production costs were cheaper in those countries but also because they could not find enough employees in Japan.

One aspect of this new scarcity of employee recruits was a significant increase in the number of foreigners allowed to come to Japan on work visas—a phenomenon that until the late 1900s was virtually unthinkable to the culturally and racially exclusive-minded Japanese.

The slow-down in the birthrate in Japan was the result of the continuing influence of traditional male-female relations and marriage in Japan. During Japan's long feudal era, which actually did not completely end until the mid-1950s, there was virtually no Western style self-arranged dating and engagements in the singles populations.

During the heyday of the feudal era love between young unmarried men and women was regarded as a hindrance to the perpetuation of the family name and was both discouraged and tabooed by various customs and laws.

KEY WORDS CONTROL YOUR LIFE!

Young Japanese females and males did not gain the social right to freely associate with members of the opposite sex until the introduction of democracy into the country in 1946, but the cultural conditioning of the past was so strong social interaction between the sexes and love matches remained rare.

Throughout the 1950s and 1960s aunts, uncles and company managers played primary roles in arranging weddings for young people. But things were changing.

The most important external factor in play during those years was the influx of American culture, which encouraged young Japanese girls to become more self-reliant, more outspoken and more in charge of their lives. They were far more susceptible to this phenomenon than their male counterparts who were shackled to their jobs and to the thinking of their parents and the older generations in general.

The social barriers between unmarried males and females remained high, limiting their dating and romancing. The median age when males and females married spiraled upward. Most female brides were in their late 20s and most grooms were in their early or mid-30s. And couples had only one or two kids.

The more freedom Japanese women had and the longer they had it the more they liked it, and the pickier they became in selecting and/or accepting mates.

This situation resulted in a array of gambits being devised by private and public organizations to get the two sexes together. Some of these ploys were based on use of the Internet; others involved sporting events.

These developments gave rise to the Japanese term *Konkatsu* [Kone-kot-sue], which translates as "Marriage Hunt"—in other words singles seeking mates. The news media naturally picked up on this term and turned it into a national campaign.

The latest sporting events to be added to the *Konkatsu* campaign were kayaking and paragliding. The ever vigilant news media explains these choices by noting that when a male and a female go kayaking or paragliding they must communicate and cooperate with each other on a very personal if not intimate level.

These actions break down most of the barriers that have traditionally kept the Japanese sexes apart. Reports are positive. Significant numbers of the paddlers and gliders have become dating couples and some marriages have resulted—an o*nly in Japan* solution.

Get Off the Beaten Track And Have a Spiritual Experience!

One of the most remarkable of the extraordinary events that resulted from the growing importance of Buddhism in Japan from the mid-6th century on was the appearance of a priest named Kukai [774-835] who founded the Shingon sect of Buddhism in 805

KEY WORDS CONTROL YOUR LIFE!

and became known as Kobo Daishi after his death—the most famous name in Japanese Buddhism.

As hundreds of itinerant Buddhist priests did during this era Kobo Daishi searched for an especially scenic place to build a temple. He found such a place on *Koyasan* [Koe-yoe-Sahn], Mt. Koya, an uplifted cedar-forested plain surrounded by eight mountain peaks on Kii Peninsula in what is now Wakayama Prefecture, near the coast east of Osaka [which at that time was known as Naniwa].

In 816 Kukai started the construction of a spectacular temple called Kongobuji in a heavily forested area of the 3,000 meter high plain, completing it in 825. The temple became the headquarters of the Shingon sect of Buddhism, which soon came to be patronized by members of the Imperial Court in Kyoto.

Other Buddhist priests were drawn to the spectacular spot and built their own temples there, turning it into the holiest place in Japan and resulting in it playing a astounding role in the history of Japan over the next 1,000 years-plus, with emperors, shoguns and provincial feudal lords as frequent visitors. The tomb of Hideyoshi Toyotomi, a peasant who rose to unify Japan and become its ruler [1585-1598], is located there, along with that of many other notables.

Early in its history the famed temple town attracted religious pilgrims and curious visitors from all over the islands and eventually had over 200,000 priests and famous historical figures buried there in a vast cemetery.

KEY WORDS CONTROL YOUR LIFE!

By the end of the Tokugawa Shogun era in the 1870's there were 117 temples on the heavily forested high-rise plain, with approximately half of them functioning as *shukubo* [shuu-kuu-boh], or temples that offer lodgings to religious pilgrims and ordinary tourists. The lodging experiences at these *shukubo* include the opportunity to participate in such traditional Buddhist practices as calligraphic copying sutras, and engaging in meditation with the guidance of temple priests.

Other activities at the *shukubo* temples include a fire ritual known as *goma* [go-mah] that is a symbolic way of burning away the excess earthly desires that build up in the human mind. This ritual is accompanied by Buddhist priests chanting sutras, giving it a mystical aura. Some of the temple lodges charge modest fees for participating in their rituals.

The purpose of the meditation ritual is to empty the mind of extraneous thoughts and focus all of one's awareness on the symbol of the primary Buddhist deity, and let the universal reality of Buddhism flow into one's life.

[Emptying the mind of all of the external thoughts that constantly assail one is not as easy as you might think. Daizetsu Suzuki, one of Japan's most famous contemporary Zen Buddhist priests whom I had the great pleasure of meeting in Kamakura before he passed away, once said that the longest he had ever been able to totally free his mind of all thoughts was one and a half seconds.

The recommended way of getting to Koyasan is by the Nankai Electric Company's Koya Line from

Namba Station in Osaka. It takes about 90 minutes to the base of the mount on a limited express train, and then a 5-minute cable car ride to the top of the mountain. There is also bus service from the base of the mountain to and within Koyasan Town.

Koyasan is an outstanding one-day side-trip from Osaka but it is more interesting to make the visit an all-nighter by staying at one of the temple-lodges. It is vital that visitors who want to stay overnight have reservations, which can be made through email at the official website of the Koyasan Tourist Association [KTA] and Shukubo Temple Lodge Association: http:eng.shukubo.net/about.html.

Koyasan continues to attract visitors, including believers and devotees, from around the world. It is also an important stop-over destination for people returning from the *"Pilgrimage to the 88 Temples of Shikoku"*—another major story in Japan's unique culture.

The Fascinating Story of Inns in Japan!

The mix of modern and traditional lifestyles in Japan is one of the most remarkable facets in the Japan experience—facets that incorporate some of the most sophisticated facilities and amenities in the world today with a lifestyle that is more than a thousand years old...and remains emotionally, intellectually and spiritually fulfilling to an amazing degree.

KEY WORDS CONTROL YOUR LIFE!

There are, in fact, many extraordinary things about Japan that the rest of the world generally knows nothing about. One of the most interesting of these things is that by the 1630s Japan had a nationwide network of inns for travelers...a network that had appeared virtually overnight.

Furthermore, all of the inns in the network— altogether numbering over 6,000 ordinary inns and over 400 luxury inns—were located specific distances apart [how far one would normally walk in one day carrying baggage] on all of the major roads in the country. These "post stations," which in effect were small villages or towns, were built around the newly constructed inns to provide a variety of other services for travelers.

This extraordinary phenomenon began in 1635 when the recently established Tokugawa Shogun government in Edo [Tokyo] decreed that some 270 of the clan lords, whose fiefs were spread around the country, would spend every other year in Edo in attendance at the Shogun's Court.

This security measure required that the clan lords maintain residences in Edo; that they keep their wives and children in Edo at all times; and that on their semiannual treks to Edo they would be accompanied by a designated number of samurai warriors and attendants, based on the size and wealth of their domains.

The Maeda lord, the richest of the fief lords, maintained four mansions in Edo with a combined staff of 10,000 people, and on his trips to Edo brought an additional 1,000 warriors and attendants with him.

KEY WORDS CONTROL YOUR LIFE!

These extraordinary troops of lords, clan staff, samurai warriors and personal attendants were known as *Daimyo Gyoretsu* (die-m'yoh g'yoh-rate-sue), or "Processions of the Lords. The dates of their travel to and from Edo, the routes they took and when and where they stopped overnight were all fixed by the Shogun.

When on the road the colorful, coordinated processions had the right of way. Ordinary people on the roads and in the villages and towns they passed through were required to get off of the road and bow down as the processions passed. Anyone failing to abide by these strict rules could be beheaded by the lords' samurai warriors.

This shogun-mandated system continued for some 240 years [until 1870], and was a primary factor in the political, social and economic life of the Japanese for all those generations!

Keeping the inns supplied with staff, food, drink and other items to accommodate the lords and their entourages—plus the hundreds of thousands of other regular travelers [businesspeople, salesmen, sumo wrestlers, entertainers and gamblers] who quickly took advantage of the network of inns, and keeping the inns and post stations in repair, was second only to agricultural in the Japanese economy.

On just the Tokaido (toe-kie-doh), or "Eastern Sea Road, between Kyoto and Edo (Tokyo), there were 111 *honjin* (hoan-jeen), or luxury inns for the lords and other high-ranking guests, 68 *waki-honjin* (wah-kee-hoan-jeen), or semi-luxury inns for the next level of travelers, and 2,905 *hatago* (hah-tah-go) inns for ordinary travelers.

A few of these historic inns still exist, and hundreds of others have survived in a succession of reincarnations.

No one can say they have fully experienced Japan until they have spent several days and nights in a traditionally styled Japanese *ryokan* (rio-kahn), or inn—especially one in an area that is so scenic it is spellbinding.

Japan Has Had a Tourism Industry For 2,000 Years!

As a result of several serendipitous geological features Japan has had a tourism industry for over two thousand years...

One of these special circumstances was the existence of Shintō, Japan's indigenous religion, which dates back to the origin of the Japanese race.

A nature-based religion that incorporates the physical and the spiritual, Shintō was imbued with the concept that there is a cosmic connection between all things and all things in nature should be revered.

This made the Japanese extremely sensitive to their natural surroundings, and to the extraordinary beauty of the islands, which is highlighted by their hills and mountains, picturesque gorges, canopy of trees, and one of the longest combined coastlines in the world

KEY WORDS CONTROL YOUR LIFE!

that are indented by thousands of incredible beautiful inlets and coves.

Very early in their history the Japanese designated a large number of these views as "Sights Fit for the Eyes of Kings," resulting in the creation of itineraries for sightseers that led to the development one of the world's first tourism industries.

Despite industrialization and the creation of a modern lifestyle most of the natural beauty of Japan remains, and the tourism industry is now undergoing a reformation that includes both its natural and historical attractions.

Local and regional governments have set goals for tripling the number of tourists—both foreign and domestic—with their sights set on 20+ million people a year.

To achieve such dramatic results plans are afoot to significantly upscale the thousands of Japanese style inns and Western style hotels around the country; and to significantly improve the variety and quality of services provided for tourists, from transportation and tour guides to a mix of the historical and modern.

Much of the impetus for this reformation has come from comments and suggestions made by tourists themselves. Virtually all tourists going to Japan have a preconceived list of things they want to see and do and they are vocal about letting tour operators and guides know,

Among the more intriguing sights for foreign as well as domestic travelers are the large number of villages, towns and city neighborhoods that have not

KEY WORDS CONTROL YOUR LIFE!

been Westernized; that are just like they were hundreds of years ago.

Another change in the Japanese travel industry is its growing ability to cater to small groups of men and women—especially single girls in their teens and twenties for they are one of the most ardent group of travelers in the country.

Foreign travelers planning a trip to Japan, whether as twosomes and threesomes or gangs of five or six should make lists prior to their arrival of what they want to see and do,

Those joining conducted tour groups should also make up lists of their wants and provide them to the tour companies handling their visits, clearly letting them know that they do not want an old standard tour.

Again, the best part of this upgrading of Japan's tourism industry is that it has become national policy—and one of the best elements in Japan's traditional culture is when they set out to do something *they do it!*

Recommended books: *JAPAN – A New Way of Getting the Most Out of a Japan Experience; JAPAN – Aspects of a Unique Culture that Attracts Foreigners; AMAZING JAPAN – Why Japan is One of the World's Most Intriguing Countries; EXOTIC JAPAN! – The Sensual & Visual Pleasures.*

KEY WORDS CONTROL YOUR LIFE!

Viewing Japan from the Top Of the World!

One of the latest and most popular adventures for foreign tourists going to Japan is climbing Mt. Fuji, recently designated a World Heritage Site. Another new attraction for foreign visitors is "vintage bike rides" around the huge waist of the mountain.

Well over 300,000 people climb Mt. Fuji each year and a growing number of these climbers are foreign visitors who come to Japan for that purpose. The climbing season is generally limited to July and August, and many people climb at night to be on top the following morning to watch the sun rise.

Temperatures at the top hover around 40 degrees F., but at night they can dip below freezing. On my last sleep-over in a crater hut at the top I ended up sleeping under five thick heavy futon quilts.

Mt. Fuji is one of the most extraordinary sights on planet Earth, especially when viewed from an airplane approaching the Japanese islands. The towering volcanic peak—3,776 meters or 12,388 feet high—is 2.34 miles above sea level and approximately 100 kilometers [60 miles] from Tokyo.

Fuji San [as it is known in Japanese] is the tallest mountain in Japan and since 1603, when the tiny village of Edo [present-day Tokyo] became the capital of the newly established Tokugawa Shogunate, it has been the most famous and honored natural view in the country.

KEY WORDS CONTROL YOUR LIFE!

Residents living in Edo and those approaching and leaving the Shogunate capital who had unobstructed views could see the snow-capped peak from as far away as 300 kilometers [180 miles], resulting in it becoming the subject of poetry and tall tales in literature going back to ancient times and a popular image on woodblock prints during the Tokugawa era.

When the great woodblock artist Hokusai traveled the famed *Tokaido* {Toe-kigh-doe] or "Eastern Sea Road" from Edo to the Imperial capital of Kyoto he was so impressed with the many views of the mountain from the road that he created two woodblock masterpiece collections: "36 Views of Mt. Fuji," and "100 Views of Mt. Fuji"—both still treasured artifacts among woodblock devotees.

From ancient times the summit of Mt. Fuji was conidered sacred in Shintō mythology, and women were not allowed to climb it until the Meiji Era [1870-1912]. The first male climber is said to have been a monk who reached the top in 663, Samurai warriors had training camps around the base of the mountain as far back as the 14th century.

The first foreigner to climb Mt. Fuji was a British diplomat named Rutherford Alcock, who made the climb in 1868. According to a book he wrote it took him eight hours [from a base camp mid-way up the mountain reached by bus] to reach the peak but he made the descent in only three hours. Descending can be a combination of running and sliding down the loose volcanic rock slope if you don't mind occasional spills—something I have done twice.

KEY WORDS CONTROL YOUR LIFE!

Lady Fanny Parkes, the wife of British ambassador Sir Harry Parkes, was the first non-Japanese woman to ascend the mountain—in 1869.

There are ten "stations" and a number of "sub-stations" from the bottom to peak. There are four starting routes from the foot of the mountain and four from the fifth station. Most climbers begin their adventure from the towns of Lake Kawaguchi, Subashiri, Gotemba or Fujinomiya, going by bus to Station Five on each of these routes.

There are huts and other facilities at each of the stations on the way up the mountain. But it pays to take snacks, a canteen of water, and your own toilet paper.

Many Tokyo area residents and visitors who climb Mt. Fuji take a train from Shinjuku Station to Fujinomiya at the foot of the mountain and then board a bus going to Station Five. As of this writing there was also direct bus service from Shinjuku to this starting point. Fujinomiya itself is an interesting stopover. The main street is in direct alignment with Mt. Fuji and offers an incredible ascending view up to its peak.

As one of the world's newest World Heritage Sites, climbing Mt. Fuji has become a real bragging point for visitors who make it to the top.

AN ONLY IN JAPAN KIND OF THING!

Since the turn of the 21st century young Japanese have begun looking back and rediscovering the role

KEY WORDS CONTROL YOUR LIFE!

that Shintō played in the history of the country—something that also provides foreign residents and visitors with a unique opportunity to see and experience a side of Japan that is unique.

This new phenomenon has been labeled *Ichinomiya* [Ee-chee-no-me-yah] by the press. The term literally means "one [first] shrine," but it connotes the shrine with the highest rank in the area. The press also created a new term for shrine-goers made up of *miya* [shrine] and *mairu* [to go or to pray], and added "er" to it to get *miya-mairer*, which is Japanese-English for "shrine-goer."

The travel industry is naturally a key player in the *ichinomiya* phenomenon, identifying the most popular shrines and their role in the origin and history of the country.

Like all ancient people the Japanese came up with a polytheistic creation myth. That is they attributed their existence and the existence of the world at large to a large number of gods—one for each of the most important things in life and in nature.

These gods were incorporated into what came to be called Shintō [Sheen-tohh], which translates as "The Way of the Kami or Gods."

But Shintō went far beyond such recent religions such as Judaism, Christianity and Islam, which are primarily concerned with the behavior of people.

In Shintō the gods pertained not only to the origin-beliefs and behavior of the people, they literally inhabited and gave spirit to all things in nature—all living creatures and all material things from mountains on down.

KEY WORDS CONTROL YOUR LIFE!

This concept gave the Japanese a unique view of themselves and the world, making them and all the things in the world kindred spirits.

The influence of this view permeated everything in the lives of the Japanese—from their arts and crafts to their view and use wood and other materials for making things. Expressed in another way, it incorporated the abstract forces of nature into all areas of human life.

Shintō had no founder, no sacred texts and no formalized system of doctrine. It was simply the essence of the culture that the Japanese developed and passed on from one generation to the next—an essence that created a unique Japanese consciousness.

The primary rule of Shintō was that people live in harmony with each other and with everything in nature—a concept expressed in the term *wa* [wah], which became the basic principle of Japan's first constitution and the foundation of government.

Beginning around 600 B.C. shrines were built in places associated with the origin of the Japanese islands and the people.

Today there are over 80,000 shrines in the country and it has long been a national custom for people to go on pilgrimages that encompassed dozens to hundreds of shrines—a custom that has been revived in recent years.

It hardly needs to be said that the ancient Shintō concept of harmony and its influence on the lives of the Japanese—especially since the end of the

KEY WORDS CONTROL YOUR LIFE!

Shogun era in 1867/70—mostly disappeared when the country began Westernizing.

But the still existing 80,000 shrines remain as a testament to the role that shrines have traditionally played in Japan and offer foreign visitors an opportunity to go back in time and both see and feel ancient Japan in settings of incredible natural beauty; places that have long been regarded as sacred and have great spiritual power.

Among the most famous of these shrines, some of which go back more than 2,000 years, are the Izumo Taisha in Shimane Prefecture, Keita Taisha in Ishikawa, Itsukushima Shrine in Hiroshima, Otori Taisha in Osaka, Omiwa in Nara and Katori Jingu in Chiba adjoining Tokyo.

Tokyo's Marunouchi district—between Tokyo Central Station and the outer park area of the Imperial Palace Grounds—has been transformed into one of Japan's most spectacular tourist attractions with high-rise office buildings that feature restaurants, shopping floors, view floors, and lobby cafes.

In the 1990's a new high-rise building was added to this complex that competes not only with the district's other high-rise towers that are virtual communities within themselves but also with the spectacular *Tokyo SkyTree* in the Asakusa district, one of the city's most popular attractions for both residents and visitors.

Marunouchi's new addition, known as the *JP Tower*, became one of the top attractions in Tokyo the day it opened. Among the things that make the new high-rise complex especially unique is that its first floor area incorporates a renovation of the *Tokyo Central*

KEY WORDS CONTROL YOUR LIFE!

Post Office, which was built in 1931 and became one of the city's landmark buildings.

At the time of its construction it was described as "a masterpiece of modernistic architecture." JP stands for "Japan Post Office."

The new JP Tower, located about 100 yards from Tokyo Central Station [which itself quickly became a tourist attraction], is a glassed in 38-storey building that houses a post office, business offices and a shopping mall with an enormous food court that includes a postal museum.

The JP shopping mall, which features a high cathedral ceiling, is known as the *Kitte Mall* [Kitte translates as "Postage Stamp]," but it is anything but small. It takes up six basement floors and features brand-name shops from all over the country, including a wide range of traditional regional handicrafts. There is also a bookstore and café in the mall. Altogether there are 98 retailers in the mall.

The sixth floor of the mall has a roof-top garden that offers a dramatic view of Tokyo Central Station next door and the surrounding area.

There is a food and beverage court known as *Kitte Granche* on the mall's basement floor. During the lunch period it swarms with workers from the tower's offices as well as adjoining buildings.

The food court has 34 eateries, of which 25 are famous-brand food outlets from other parts of the country...the idea being that Tokyo residents and visitors can now sample numerous famous regional dishes in one location. [During Japan's long feudal shogunate era—1192-1870—the country was divided

KEY WORDS CONTROL YOUR LIFE!

into some 270 semi-independent fiefs, most of which had their own distinctive products and dishes.]

There are 15 restaurants on the fifth and sixth floors. One of these places is a conveyor-belt sushi restaurant that is operated by the famous Nemuro-hana-maru Hokkaido sushi chain.

For the convenience of visitors arriving in the district by train there is a subterranean walkway from Tokyo Central Station to the JP Tower. There is also a shop-lined underground passageway from the opposite side of Tokyo Central Station to Chuo [Central] Street, at the north end of the Ginza, a famous shopping and entertainment district that has been considered the center of Tokyo since the 1880s.

There are similar "community towers" in several of Tokyo's other famous shopping and entertainment districts, including Roppongi, Shibuya, Shimbashi and Shinjuku as well as at the central train stations of most major cities in the country.

In combination with the refurbished Tokyo Central Station the JP Tower and the surrounding community towers have made this area a key destination for both out-of-town residents and the throngs of foreign visitors who descend upon Tokyo daily.

Branch of Tokyo SkyTree Sprouts Beer Pubs

Beer drinkers and people who just want to see and experienced one of the most spectacular attractions in any country should not miss the *World Beer*

KEY WORDS CONTROL YOUR LIFE!

Museum, located on the seventh floor of the Tokyo Salamachi commercial building, attached to Tokyo Skytree in Tokyo's Sumida Ward.

The *World Beer Museum* is far more than just a museum of world beers. It is also one of Japan's most spectacular beer pubs—actually it is several pubs in one, including a German pub, a Belgian pub and a UK pub.

Operated by World Liquor Importers, these pubs sell more than 500 varieties of beer from around the world along with a wide variety of ethnic foods from Germany, Belgium and elsewhere. An attached store sells some 40 varieties of limited-edition beers, including a SkyTree label.

The décor and overall atmosphere of the "beer museum" is worth a visit, even if you don't drink beer. But not trying at least one of the famous German varieties would be a great mistake. Employees of the pubs are dressed and trained to add to the ambiance of this extraordinary place.

And if you have not yet experienced Tokyo's one-of-a-kind SkyTree you can have two extraordinary experiences on the same outing. SkyTree is a combination broadcasting, restaurant and obser-vation tower that opened in 2012.

At 2,080 feet it one of the tallest towers in the world, and has architectural features and visitor attractions that are also literally out of this world.

Tokyo SkyTree was constructed by Tobu Railway Company and six broadcasters headed by NHK,

KEY WORDS CONTROL YOUR LIFE!

Japan's premiere broadcasting company, replacing Tokyo Tower as the most iconic image in the city.

The SkyTree has a series of decks at increasingly higher altitudes, the highest one at 450 meters, with fifteen feet high glass walls that provide a 360 degree view of Tokyo and the surrounding areas—including Japan's most famous view icon, the peak of Mt. Fuji some 60 miles away. Access to this view deck is by a glass tube.

Each of the view decks features distinctive attractions that offer one-of-a-kind experiences. In a number of areas the novel use of glass gives the impression that you are walking on air.

For those who may be afraid of heights, the SkyTree is based on the most advanced and sophisticated "seismic proofing" in the world, with "dampers" designed to absorb fifty percent of any earthquake.

In fact, Japan was apparently the first country in the world to develop anti-earthquake technology...with buildings constructed as far back as the Nara era (710-784) when it was the capital of Japan that have withstood hundreds of severe quakes.

One of these buildings, the huge Todaiji Temple built in 743, houses the world's largest gilded bronze image of Buddha which stands as high as a 5-story building.

As of this writing there are four ways to purchase tickets to TOKYO SKYTREE Observation Decks.

1."TOKYO SKYTREE Web tickets" may be purchased in advance online. But only credit cards issued in Japan are accepted for online reservations.

KEY WORDS CONTROL YOUR LIFE!

2. Tickets from May 22 to July 10 are by Advance Reservation Only. No day tickets will be sold during this period. Day tickets go on sale from July 11.

3. "TOKYO SKYTREE Group Reservation Center" accepts reservations for groups of 25 or more.

4. It is also possible to reserve tickets through the travel plans of various travel agencies and the accommodation plans offered by TOKYO SKYTREE Official hotels...TOKYO SKYTREE Friendship Hotels.

Oshiage Station, the "official train station" for SkyTree, adjoins the complex on the west side. It is accessible from several major station hubs in Tokyo, including Tokyo Central Station. At Tokyo Station, take the JR Sobu Rapid Line and transfer at Kinshicho to the Tokyo Metro Hanzomon Subway Line. Total time: 16 minutes.

For more about the Skytree go to www.tokyo-skytree.jp.en, the official website. It includes additional ticket information and a guide to the view decks.

High-Tech Advances Turn Toilets Into Suites Fit for Royalty!

An aspect of Japan that continues to impress and amaze visitors is the high-tech evolution of the toilet—or "restroom" in more genteel terms—from a

KEY WORDS CONTROL YOUR LIFE!

hole or slit in the floor to stylish high-tech suites that, to use an old phrase, are fit for a king or queen.

Beginning around 2006 new office buildings, department stores and even roadside rest-stop facilities and private schools began to feature upscale toilets that are the epitome of both high-tech and high-design, so much so that many of them actually attract visitors who don't have "to go"....who just want to see and marvel at them.

Among the most conspicuous example of these new restroom suites are those on the different floors of the rebuilt Daimaru Department Store, adjoining Tokyo Central Station on the east side.

Each of the basement floors as well as all of the 12 stories above ground of the famous landmark department store have restroom suites that are designed to "fit" or "suit" the products and services sold on that floor—ranging from foodstuffs on the first basement level to "Restaurant Row" on the 12th floor.

Men using urinals in the restroom suite on this floor have spectacular panoramic views of the surrounding area. The women's restroom could be compared to a presidential suite.

These new lavatories are not just "smart" in their use of high-tech, they are also designed to be "green" in their use of energy and the overall impact they have on the environment. This includes using natural lighting with electric lights that go on, automatically, only after the natural light begins to fade in the evenings.

KEY WORDS CONTROL YOUR LIFE!

A highway rest-stop facility for women maintained by Metropolitan Express Company in Kawaguchi north of Tokyo looks like something you would find in a ritziest hotel, and is outfitted with a deodorization system as well as a system that emits aromatherapy oil.

Said a spokesperson for Metropolitan Express Company: "Restrooms that help tired drivers relax and renew themselves just make good sense"—a rationale that is, of course, perfectly rational, but is something that one generally finds only in Japan.

The movement in Japan to rethink and redesign restrooms is rapidly becoming a standard among Japan's managers who see it as yet another way to raise the corporate image of their companies while contributing to the greening of the country.

Not surprisingly, this movement has given birth to a growing number of firms that specialize in designing toilets. One of the most prominent of these firms is Gondola Architects, which designed the restrooms of Daimaru Department Store. Another prominent toilet designer is Yasui Architects & Engineers Inc.

This phenomenon, which is apparently unique to Japan, is a clear manifestation of Japanese culture—not just a commercial ploy to burnish the image of companies.

The Japanese are culturally imbued with both the desire and the need to design and create things that incorporate the concepts of elegance and beauty as well as function—elements that are characteristic of all of their traditional arts and crafts.

KEY WORDS CONTROL YOUR LIFE!

This national trait is, of course, one of the primary reasons why the Japanese have been so successful in designing and manufacturing such a large variety of consumer products that have become worldwide bestsellers—a design influence that has had a fundamental impact on product designers around the world.

There are, in fact, over 50 key principles of traditional Japanese designs that I have identified and explained in my book, *ELEMENTS OF JAPANESE DESIGN— Key Terms for Understanding & Using Japan's Classic Wabi-Sabi-Shibui Concepts.*

These design elements constitute the whole framework of Japan's traditional culture, from the principle of *wa* (wah), or harmony, to the philosophy of Zen— which teaches one to recognize the difference between illusion and reality.

So the next time you are in Tokyo and have occasion to visit a high-end (no pun intended!) toilet in Daimaru, the NEC Tamagawa Renaissance City or NEC's new headquarters building in Tokyo's Minato War, the Kinrankai Girl's School in Osaka, or any of dozens of other new buildings throughout the country be aware that they are not just gimmicks. They are reflections of Japanese culture.

THE END OF THE GOD MYTH!

Religions have played a vital role in human life since the earliest days of the species as an attempt by hu-

KEY WORDS CONTROL YOUR LIFE!

mans to come to terms with their existence, with nature and all the natural phenomena.

The earliest humans believed there was a "god" for humans as well as everything else in nature.

However, the recent history of religions and gods is one of the most sordid and shocking elements in the history of mankind—despite the good intentions built into them by their male founders.

Many intelligent people have clearly understood for several generations that there is no such thing as a god, but even today millions of people profess to believe in the existence of a supreme God…and most of those who know better are afraid to admit it in public.

But in a fantastic break with the past the new Pope in Rome, Pope Francis, publicly announced in October 2014 that there is no God in the traditional sense.

The new Pope, the 266th in the reign of Popes, is an Argentina-born Italian Catholic named Jorge Mario Bergoglio who is not only intelligent but is brave beyond words!

In his October 2014 statement Pope Francis acknowledged that the earth and human beings are products of natural evolution over ages of time.

But belief in a God still controls the attitudes and behavior of several billion people today because human beings are like robots. They can be programmed to believe in anything.

KEY WORDS CONTROL YOUR LIFE!

And the concept of a God is so deeply embedded in the mindset of Jews, Christians and Muslims that it is an integral part of their speech and in popular slogans like "In God We Trust!"

The One-God Concept

From ancient to virtually modern times all societies had a variety of gods, some numbering in the dozens. While some of the gods had to do with the origin of life, others were the gods of such natural phenomena as the wind, the oceans and mountains.

Jews Create Yahweh/God

Between three and four thousand years ago the religious leaders of the Israelites [Hebrews], a group of Semite tribes who lived in the area of what is now modern Israel, came up with the idea that just one all-powerful god would be far better than many gods, so they decided to worship only one god, whom they referred to as Yahweh.

As time passed the Hebrews began to claim that Yahweh was the *only* God and that all who did not believe in and worship him were doomed to go to Hell when they died. Their religion came to be known as Judaism [from the name of one of the Israelite tribes], and its members came to be known as Jews.

The creators of Yahweh [God] knew absolutely nothing about the Earth or world at large, including the many civilizations around the globe and the billions of galaxies and trillions of stars [suns] that make up the universe.

KEY WORDS CONTROL YOUR LIFE!

So they had no problem in attributing all things in life and nature to their new God, including the belief that creation occurred only a few thousand years earlier—which was as far back as the Jewish people could trace their ancestry.

The Jesus Christ Add-On

Several centuries after the concept of one god became well established in Jewish culture the descendants of the creators of Yahweh took bits and pieces from many other religions—including the concept of virgin birth—and came up with the idea that more people would believe in and worship their God if he sent them a son as his personal go-between

This gave birth to the Biblical story of Mary and her son who later became known as Jesus Christ the Savior of mankind. [The word "Christ" comes from the Greek term meaning "oil."—with which the Jews bathed the feet of those they regarded as holy.]

The Spread of Christianity

Over the next few hundred years the one-God cult of the Jews morphed into the theological and social cult that came to be known as Christianity, which eventually was split into Catholicism, Protestantism and a mish-mash of other sects, including Mormonism, by males who did not accept all of the teachings of the Catholic Church and had their own ideas of God's will and the proper behavior of men and women.

KEY WORDS CONTROL YOUR LIFE!

While the original aim of Christianity—whose founding is often credited to the Jewish tribal leader Abraham—was to assert and maintain human worth and dignity it was soon subverted into a tribal identity and competed with other faiths for social and political power.

Thus the numerous wars waged in the name of Christianity and its offshoots over the millennia and down to modern times.

Still today most Christian sects, especially Catholicism, are basically tribal religions that traditionally served the interests of their male founders and administrators at the expense of females and competing religions—a stark revelation of the ignorance and willful stupidity of the founders and subsequent leaders.

Still to give credit where it is due, the more recent generations of Catholic leaders have mitigated some of their feudal male concepts and introduced some rationality into their beliefs and teachings.

There is no more stark evidence of the inhumanity of the bigoted god-based Catholicism of the past as the invasion and conquering of the New World in the 1500s by Spanish conquistadors who believed that their Catholic religious beliefs took precedence over the cultures and lives of the millions of people who lived on the Caribbean Islands and the North and South American continents.

The conquistadors believed that since the natives were not Catholic killing them was justified.

KEY WORDS CONTROL YOUR LIFE!

God's Terrible Swift Sword!

In America's Civil War [1861-1865] in which hundreds of thousands of young men were killed and more hundreds of thousands of others were horribly mutilated both the North and South sides publicly and loudly proclaimed that God was on their side and that they were doing God's work.

Southerners justified their keeping of black human beings as slaves as in keeping with the will of God. Northerners justified their going to war as a fight against evil and sang about "God's terrible swift sword" helping them vanquish the Southern rebels.

In the mid-1800's the United States government initiated military campaigns against Native American Indians, whom it regarded as pagan savages with few if any rights. The campaigns were designed to round up the Indians and confine them to Reservations. Large numbers of those who resisted were killed. This campaign did not end until the 1880s.

Native Americans were called Indians because the European who discovered the Caribbean Islands [Christopher Columbus] thought he had reached India, the source of spices so highly valued by Europeans. He intended to establish a. direct route for importing them.

It was not until 1924 that Native American Indians, whose ancestors had lived here for thousands of years, were "granted" citizenship by the government that had conspired in killing most of them and depriving most of the survivors of their traditional homelands.

What a travesty, and what an indictment against the religious beliefs and practices of early European-Americans.

Another thing few White Americans know is that when the Navajo Indians of Arizona were first contacted by Whites [Spaniards in the early 1600's] their culture was far more sophisticated and far more humane than the culture of the Whites. Furthermore, an extraordinary devotion to the arts and to poetry was a universal trait among the Navajos...something you could not say even about percent of the Whites.

The Power of the God Cult

In earlier times the power of the cult of Christianity and its off-shoots to seduce and hold the minds of the most educated men and women was to shape the future of their followers in ways that could not have been intended—causing, death, destruction and incredible suffering on a massive scale.

Since creation of Yahweh/God the knowledge that human beings have learned about the universe, its origin and how it works, is off the scale, and yet millions of educated people continue to profess belief in the God-concept taught by Judaism, Christianity, Islam and all of their offshoots, and to worship a God who represents all of the elements in the nature of human males, the good and the bad—a form of willful stupidity that is pathological to the extreme.

KEY WORDS CONTROL YOUR LIFE!

The only thing more incredible than this ongoing pathological reverence for an imaginary God are the rationales that believers in Judaism, Christianity and Islam use to convince themselves and others that there *is* a God who created everything some five or six thousand year ago and is responsible for everything, despite the obvious evidence to the contrary.

Historically, Jews, Christians and Moslems have slaughtered each other while shouting that God is on their side. When tragic things occur they say it is God's will, while continuing to preach that God is the ultimate guardian and protector of human beings and will save people from evil and disaster if they believe in him and pray to him—or his "son," the young Jew Jesus…who ended up being crucified by the Romans who regarded his teachings as rebellious rhetoric.

What is now just as incredible is that many people *know* that belief in a benign God creator and protector is absolute nonsense but most of them—especially politicians—are afraid to publicly admit it.

What was weirdly amusing at the turn of the 21st century was that one of the few individuals with a public pulpit who was not afraid to speak the truth about the God fable was a comedian: Bill Maher, the host of *Real Time* on HBO. Bill repeatedly said the God story was BS--just nonsense.

Promoting and Selling God

Since around 500 A.D. the God fable has become a major industry, and today its various constituents employ several million people. These include managers of institutions like the Catholic Church, Jewish

KEY WORDS CONTROL YOUR LIFE!

synagogues and Islamic mosques along with a large number of individuals who use the airwaves to con people into sending them money.

Of course, Jewish, Christian and Islamic sects and their hundreds of thousands of churches provide some material support for many of members, but their use of the God fable to attract and hold these members is indefensible.

In addition to perpetrating a false faith these institutions provide people with a way of avoiding personal responsibility for their behavior. The fact that these faiths allow their members to slaughter each other in the name of and for their God is a form of insanity.

The radio and television babble of many of the religious con men and con women is so infantile, so stupid, so obviously put-on, that only people who have been programmed to the moronic level could actually believe what they say and send them money.

The efforts of obviously well-educated members of the Catholic Church and similar organizations to affirm the existence of a Creator-God are marvelous demonstrations of their skill with words in "proving" something for which there is absolutely no evidence and vast amounts of evidence to the contrary.

What is most disturbing and the most dangerous for humanity is that equally well-educated and knowledgeable people in positions of great power and influence cop-out by agreeing with or pretending to agree with the God people.

KEY WORDS CONTROL YOUR LIFE!

By this time it should be obvious to all that the most destructive element in God-based moralities is the fact that they are male-oriented and male-dominated.

If you are interested in and/or concerned about this destructive influence see the books *THE PLAGUE OF MALE DOMINANCE* and *THE ORIGINS OF HUMAN VIOLENCE*

If Gods Were Actually in Charge!

If gods were actually in charge of human nature and had any control over human behavior you certainly would not expect them to complicate their responsibility by making men and women so sexual...and then allow their Earthly agents to create extraordinary barriers designed to prevent men and women from engaging in sex at will...even labeling sex a mortal sin except under carefully prescribed circumstances that favored men!

No matter which way or how often this male-designed and ruled world is white-washed it is both irrational and inhuman.

Of course, there were enough valid social and political reasons for male leaders of early societies and religions to curb the sexual behavior of men and women. But the way they went about it was both inhuman and cruel. First of all, they put most of the blame on women, accusing them of not being able to

KEY WORDS CONTROL YOUR LIFE!

control their sexual nature and therefore being a clear and present danger to society.

Some of the measures promoted or condoned by the Christian Church during the so-called Middle Ages to control female sexual behavior are hardly believable today.

Beginning in the 11th century, European Christian leaders launched a series of religious-inspired military campaigns against Middle East countries in an attempt to free Jerusalem and the other "Holy Cities" from their Moslem occupiers.

These so-called Crusades against Islamic countries continued for approximately three hundred years.

During this incredibly long period of pope-and-king backed wars some men had their wives outfitted with chastity belts—iron thong-like devices that were locked in place to prevent the women from being able to have sexual intercourse with other males while the husbands were away doing their religious duty.

Most of these lockable iron chastity belts|| were apparently made in Italy, where their manufacture and use was promoted by the Catholic Church.

Even farther out than this device was an older practice among ancient slave holders to have the foreskin of the penises of their adult male slaves sewn tight, leaving only a tiny hole for urination, to discourage them from engaging in sexual intercourse with any woman—another extreme to which men have gone in the past to control sex-ual behavior.

KEY WORDS CONTROL YOUR LIFE!

Ironically, most of the glory-hungry knights who left Europe in their zeal to capture the Holy Land never returned home. Some 20 percent of them were killed in battle, and some 60 or 70 percent of them died from the plague and other diseases.

History also notes, not surprisingly, that many women managed to get around the iron chastity belts by one means or another, including having a second key made by willing locksmiths.

According to a number of totally unreliable sources on the Internet some form of chastity belts continued to be used in Europe well after the end of the Crusades, and, in fact, into modern times. Such is the terrible hold that religious beliefs have on both men and women.

Sex in Godless Societies

The suppression and control of female sexuality by males has not been limited to god-based societies. It is a basic instinct in the genetic makeup of males, and while the customs and practices have differed somewhat in godless and god-based societies they have essentially been the same.

As already noted, there have been conspicuous exceptions to this rule in some isolated island societies, and in earlier times there were groups in large societies such as India, where sexual intercourse with multiple partners was seen and practiced as a ritual—as a form of piety. I think the Romans did it simply because it relieved sexual tensions, made them feel good, and was fun.

KEY WORDS CONTROL YOUR LIFE!

This latter rationale is has been growing rapidly among young generations around the world but it still has a long way to go.

Sex around the World

In today's world the sexual customs of people range from the primitive practices of Islamic countries to the free-for-alls that one finds on many college campuses in the U.S. and else-where.

Among many devout people in god-based societies the practices have not changed very much since ancient times. Women in this category are still required to suppress their sexuality, while many men still feel it is their god-given right to have sex with multiple partners.

But in such nominal god-based societies as the United States the sexual behavior of most people is no longer controlled by any religious beliefs they may have. It is more a matter of their personal inclination, economic and social status, opportunity, and soon.

But the problem of human sexuality is far from solved and continues to have a seriously negative impact on the mental and physical health of both men and women. The sexual needs of the average male and female are far from being met. The unused sexual energy that builds up, that is constantly fanned by incredibly powerful images on television and in movies, remains a bomb ticking away in the psyche of people.

By the time the average male is 60 years old he has had some 60,000 thousand unused hard-ons. The stress this causes is the reason for the problems older males have with enlarged prostate glands.

As noted elsewhere, it was not until the late 1800's and early 1900's that professional male researchers finally discovered and admitted that females have a powerful sex-drive and that stimulation results in a sexual climax.

How Males Put a Kink In the Sex Life of Both Sexes!

The first civilizations created by human beings put a kink in the sexual monopoly of big strong males. After the advent of larger organized societies most men, officially at least and finally because of the influence of some women, were required to limit themselves to just one official mate at a time.

But in most societies males made sure they still had access to mistresses, concubines, harems and prostitutes.

Then along came Judaism, Christianity and Islam—all of which were created and controlled by men and all of which established—god-given—laws controlling the sexual behavior of men and women, with the laws naturally skewered in favor of men. In these male-created and controlled religions females were a godly afterthought, created to serve men.

As time went by, overly zealous Christian popes and theologians—all males and often men who didn't like

KEY WORDS CONTROL YOUR LIFE!

women—began to preach that women were naturally evil and would seduce and debase men if they had the slightest opportunity.

They then created a world in which women had to deny and suppress their sexuality, resulting in indescribable frustration and suffering to the point that mental and physical ailments among women became common.

And, of course, in Moslem societies the ruling clerics (in the name of god, of course), sanctioned the primitive alpha male concept of sexual behavior, allowing men to have several wives and to treat women in general as inferior shadows, not to be seen or heard.

What the ancient world's alpha males and all of the religious clerics, ministers, popes, priests, shamans, or whatever they are called misunderstood or ignored was the fundamental sexual nature of human beings.

These misguided and ego-driven men denied or ignored the fact that among all members of the animal kingdom, including human beings, sexuality comes right after survival in the built-in gene-powered drive of all living things.

Furthermore, human beings, unlike some of our lower-order relatives, are "in heat" all the time. This especially applies to normal males and to females but in the case of the latter that are so many civilization and religious oriented restraints on females that until the 21st century most of them were forced by the power of males to limit their sexual behavior to very narrowly prescribed situations

KEY WORDS CONTROL YOUR LIFE!

HOW TO SELECT HOT MATES INSTEAD OF COLD FISH!

Your face reveals your sexual nature! Everybody reads faces from day one, but few people become skilled at reading all of the information broad-cast by the facial features. In many ways, your face is your fortune—not only in the friends you make and keep but especially in what you do for a living and the mates and playmates you choose—and/or that choose you!

The shape of your skull, your forehead, your eyebrows, eyes, nose, lips, mouth, chin and ears, all broadcast messages about your built-in sexuality – how cool or how hot you are, and so on.

Chinese physicians cataloged the primary readings of the human face more than 3,000 years ago, including the sexual connotations of the different features, eventually institutionalizing face-reading as an important skill for business people, for government officials, for military officers and finally for ordinary men and women who wanted to take most of the guess-work out of picking mates and playmates. The art was imported into Japan around 1400 A.D.

I studied the art in China and Japan in the 1950s and in the 1960s wrote a book, *Face-Reading for Fun & Profit*. It has since been republished as *ASIAN FACE READING – Unlock the Secrets Hidden in the Human Face*.

KEY WORDS CONTROL YOUR LIFE!

I have extracted all of the key sexuality-oriented readings from that book and published it as *How to Measure the Sexuality of Men & Women by their Facial Features.*

Some of the readings are obvious. Many are not. If you would like to improve your chances of selecting a mate or playmate with a good built-in sex drive... especially if it is your second or third time around, this book will give you a leg up. It is available from Amazon.

There has historically been specific groups of people who were superior to the average groups in many ways—intellectually, technically, creatively and otherwise. These groups include Jews, Germans and Japanese.

I detail why the Japanese are superior in my book, **Why the Japanese Are a Superior People**, available from Amazon.

It identifies and dissects the cultural factors that created the traditional character of the Japanese and gave them a long list of skills that were responsible for their amazing success in developing the world's second largest economy in less than thirty years following the debacle of World War II.

These skills include:

- Thinking Holistically!
- Mastering Forms & Processes!
- Producing Quality Goods!
- Building Sensual Appeal into Products!
- Emphasizing Emotional Intelligence!

KEY WORDS CONTROL YOUR LIFE!

Passed by China in 2010, Japan remains one of the most powerful industrial countries in the worlds, thanks to the traditional mindset and skills of the Japanese...enhanced by their ability to use both sides of their brains.

The book, available from Amazon in both digital and printed editions, identifies and explains the cultural factors that went into the mindset of the Japanese and continues to control much of their thinking and behavior. It provides valuable lessons for anyone who aspires to improve their character and chances for success in life.

WHAT YOU CAN LEARN FROM THE MEXICAN MIND!

When Americans think of great cultural achievements they generally think of Europe; when they think of the exotic and perhaps the erotic they think of the Orient...missing the fact that Mexico, their next door neighbor, also gave birth to some of the world's greatest historical achievements and today has one of the world's most unusual and fascinating cultures.

In my book, **THE MEXICAN MIND – Understanding & Appreciating Mexican Culture**, I use key "code words" in the Mexican language to identify and explain the gentle humility of poor farmers, the warmth, kindness and compassion of the average city dwellers and the extreme sensuality of the Mexican lifestyle.

KEY WORDS CONTROL YOUR LIFE!

Despite the harsh treatment inflicted upon the Mexican people by dictatorial governments over the generations they developed an astounding commitment to the arts and to dancing, music and singing that continues to distinguish them and make Mexico a fascinating country.

The book also explains why Mexicans are so attached to the culture despite its shortcomings and why so many foreigners find it so seductive and satisfying they prefer to live there.

Cultural insights in the book provide valuable guidelines for businesspeople, law enforcement agencies, students, teachers and travelers. It is available from Amazon.com in both digital and printed formats.

WHY ORIENTAL GIRLS ATTRACT WESTERN MEN!

This book, available from Amazon, provides a detailed account of the charms of Oriental girls that continue to attract, impress and seduce Western men, beginning with Marco Polo....by an author who has been there and done that!

It covers Chinese, Japanese, Korean, Thai, Vietnamese and Filipino girls. It is available in both digital and printed editions. The most important element in the sexual mindset and behavior of Oriental girls is that in their culture sex is a natural and necessary function of human behavior. Japanese men away from home were expected to indulge in sex with other women in order to remain in good health.

KEY WORDS CONTROL YOUR LIFE!

The book also contains a number of pointers that Western women might want to pick up on to enhance their feminine appeal.

World's Cultures Mired in Muck of Ignorance, Stupidity and Violence!

Throughout human history there have always been elements of ignorance and stupidity in the mindset and behavior of leaders in all fields—from business and politics to religions—and this cultural failure has resulted in incredible violence and suffering that has afflicted most of mankind since day one.

I attempt to deal with this cultural failure in my book *Why Ignorance, Stupidity and Violence Plague Mankind!*

Deep-seated beliefs that grow out of tribalism, territorialism, race, skin color, religions and selfish interests have so divided human beings that still today these factors are major elements in all areas of life.

In many people these elements override logic, objectivity and rationality in both subtle and obvious ways, resulting in behavior that, by every measure, is negative instead of positive, disruptive instead of harmonizing and destructive instead of constructive.

Examples of irrational, illogical and harmful behavior are so deeply ingrained in the minds of many people that they have become institutionalized and ritualized

KEY WORDS CONTROL YOUR LIFE!

in customs and laws and have persisted since the dawn of human history because people with invested interests in them have made sure that they continue to survive.

However, all of this is in the process of changing for the first time in history and there is now hope for humanity.

The business, political and religious Institutions that have traditionally molded and controlled the mindset and behavior of people are losing their hold on humanity because of technology that is exposing their abuse and misuse of power to the public at large and making it possible for the people to fight back..

In the U.S. one institution that is already virtually bankrupt is the multiple-party system of running governments that is based on the influence of money and self-interest.

The weaknesses and failings of this system are so obvious they don't have to be named. Members of the system will not reform it. That will take the voice and actions of the public.

Another institution whose power over the beliefs and behavior of people is waning is that of religion, particularly those that are cults in the true sense of the term—including god-based religions such as Judaism, Christianity and Islam.

But as long as these religions provide a rationale for the inhuman and irrational behavior of people, along with freeing them from being responsible for their actions, the bulk of humanity cannot become rational in mindset or behavior.

The only true hope for humanity is a universal set of beliefs that reflect the true nature of life and the cosmos at large—and that new technology can be and may be the means by which this will hap-pen.

I address all of these problems in detail in *Why Ignorance, Stupidity and Violence Plague Mankind!*, and make a series of suggestions on how humanity can at last achieve the goal of reforming itself.

Like all of my other titles the book is available from Amazon

MOTHER INDIA!
An Astounding Historical Debt Most People Know Nothing About!

Most educated people believe that the modern world owes a historical debt to Greek, Roman and Egyptian wise men for setting humanity on the road to en-lightenment—that awareness of and a growing knowledge about such topics as the Earth, the Sun, the Solar system, the stars, philosophies, religions, science etc. begin to flower some 5,000 years ago among this tiny segment of humanity.

They are all wrong!

Virtually every scrap of knowledge that eventually led to modern times and a basic understanding of the

KEY WORDS CONTROL YOUR LIFE!

universe did not begin in the mid-East, in Europe, in Africa, or in the Americas.

It began in India!

From around 8000 B.C. until the beginning of 1800 A.D. India was the planet's largest, richest and most advanced civilization, and virtually every category of learning that developed in Europe and elsewhere in the world came from India via traveling scholars.

Much of the astounding civilization that developed in India some 10,000 years ago is attributed by some to the fact that the primary language of the country was logical and nourished critical thinking on the fundamental elements of nature and mankind. That may be true but it is far too facile an explanation.

From ancient times to 1800 A.D. the wealth in India was more than twice that of the rest of the world combined. Most of the foundations of today's most advanced societies—science, medicine, mathematics, metaphysics, religion and astronomy—originated in India.

In the words of Indian historian and scholar Tejraj M. Aminabhavi, India was the cradle of human civilization, the birthplace of speech, the mother of history and numerous languages, the grand-mother of legends and traditions, and more.

Indians invented the zero and the number sys-tem, one of the greatest inventions in history. The decimal system, the value of pi, algebra, trigonometry, calculus and many mathematical concepts were all born in India.

KEY WORDS CONTROL YOUR LIFE!

The largest numbers Greeks and Romans used was 10 to the power of 6.

Long before that—well before 5000 B.C.—Indians were using numbers as big as 10 to the power of 53. Albert Einstein once noted that without the math developed in India few scientific discoveries could have been made.

Basic medicine that is practiced today was developed in ancient India. This included detailed knowledge of anatomy, embryology, digestion, metabolism, physiology, genetics, immunity, psychology and etiology.

Astronomy and metaphysics were advanced in India a thousand years before they became known to a few in the rest of the world. Most of the knowledge known today by scholars about the Earth, the solar system and the stars was known in India 4,500 years ago.

Ancient Western scholars whose names are known to the educated [Plato, Thales and Pythagoras] got their knowledge from India, directly or indirectly.

Virtually all of the ancient arts and practices now associated with China—[yoga, chess, Buddhism, ladders, buttons, steel, navigation, playing cards, gymnasiums, universities, rocket artillery, geometrical instruments, cotton, jute, martial arts, mining—all had their roots in India—introduced into China by Indian masters.

KEY WORDS CONTROL YOUR LIFE!

THE ORIGIN OF BUDDHISM IN INDIA

The origin of Buddhism in India ages ago and the development of Zen as a refinement was one of the great philosophical advances in the history of mankind.

From India Buddhism/Zen was introduced into China, then into Korea and finally into Japan, where it found a home. Japan's ruling samurai warriors made Zen the foundation of their code of behavior, creating one of the most remarkable classes of people on the planet.

My book LIVING ZEN tells the story of Zen and the 13 principles and 13 practices that Japan's most famous samurai warrior created and lived by in one of the most remarkable lives in the history of man.

It briefly relates the story of Zen in India, China, Korea and Japan, and then presents the principles and practices that detail the attributes that are needed to have a fully developed mature mindset and succeed in life.

It is a valuable guide for success in social relationships, in sports, in business, in politics…in every human endeavor. LIVING ZEN and over 70 of my other titles are available from Amazon and other online booksellers.

KEY WORDS CONTROL YOUR LIFE!

INDIA PROVIDED THE ROOTS OF CHINESE CIVILIZATION

Prehistoric Chinese civilization dates back to 7,600 B.C. By 4,000 B.C. China had adopted technology and knowhow from India that made it the second most sophisticated culture on the planet—with a rudimentary writing system, the cultivation of silk for use in making garments for the well-to-do, and the use of agricultural tools such as the plow.

By 2,350 B.C. major engineering projects were being undertaken to tame the rivers, and many of the arts and crafts that were to distinguish Chinese culture from then on had become common.

Over the next millennia China extended its military hegemony far and wide. The government of the leading state was centralized, with the concept of the "Central Kingdom" becoming a major element of the culture. One of the pastimes that became popular was the sophisticated board game of *weiqi* [way-chee], which later became well known outside of China by its Japanese name: *go*.

In 486 B.C. construction was begun on the Grand Canal of China. The diversity and sophistication of Chinese culture virtually exploded from this era on, with remarkable advances in technology, astronomy, literature, mathematics, medicine, music, education

KEY WORDS CONTROL YOUR LIFE!

of the elite, publishing, shipbuilding, military equipment, exploration, and contact with other countries.

The history of the Chinese as "the Romans of Asia" continued until the early 1500s A.D. when Europeans made their first appearance on the scene.

By that time the leaders of China had begun to take the position that China had achieved the epitome of civilization and culture and did not need to change anything, especially learn any-thing from Western "barbarians."

This concept was to eventually bring about the demise of the "Central Kingdom," as the newly industrialized powers of Europe began to carve the country up into pieces, culminating in the invasion of the country in the early 1930s by Japan.

China did not begin to recover until the arrival of the great revolutionary Zedong Mao in the early 20th century and his take-over of the country in 1949.

Mao's dream of resurrecting and rebuilding the Central Kingdom was flawed by the extremes of his ideology and despite some admirable changes [he gave women the right to vote] he virtually destroyed the country, and it was not until he died in 1976 that Xiaoping Deng, a former ally who had been disgraced and exiled, became the paramount leader and adopted the policy that "To get rich is glorious!" – in other words imitate the West.

Deng established policies that freed the Chinese population for the first time in the history of the country to utilize their incredible motivation to do

KEY WORDS CONTROL YOUR LIFE!

exactly that…to get as rich as possible—in this case by taking advantage of the profit morality of the West; exactly the same thing the Japanese had done between 1952 and 1970.

As soon as China opened its doors, American and European businessmen began importing Western products made in China and moving their own production to China. The rest, as the saying goes, is history. Much of the wealth of the United States was transferred to Chinese ownership.

By 2010 China had emerged on the world scene as a major economic and political force that now appears destined to surpass the United States—a portent of the future that goes well beyond any-thing the U.S. has faced before.

The business practices of today's China are a mixture of traditional values and customs com-bined with Western concepts and practices that, despite bumps in the highway, are propelling the country forward at warp speed.

I have attempted to address both the traditional and modern-day aspects of how business is done in China in my Amazon book *CHINA: Understanding & Dealing with the Chinese Way of Doing Business*.

In addition to offering insights in how to deal with China's hybrid [Chinese-Western] cultural and ethical business system, the book also covers aspects of China's appearance on the international scene and the globalization of its economy that is political in nature and will have an increasingly powerful impact on the rest of the world.

KEY WORDS CONTROL YOUR LIFE!

THE NEW GOD!
The Rise of Money Morality

The fact that Judaism, Christianity and Islam have failed in their self-declared mandates to control human behavior allowed the rise of a new morality that is even more destructive—a new morality that was fueled by the Industrial Revolution that began in England in the early 1800s and was to have more far-reaching effects on human history than any other element since the development of agriculture and the creation of god-based religions.

One of the most important of these effects was that the new economy that developed over the next century was centered on profit-making as the new imperative of all businesses and government organizations, and earning money was the new imperative of the people who worked for them.

During the early 19th century money and-profit-making became the economic, social and political foundations of the industrialized countries of the West. By the beginning of the 20th century all of the domestic and international affairs of the newly industrialized countries were based on the new money morality.

Both politicians and business people in the 1700's perceived and real need for economic expansion, both to meet growing populations and the hunger for more economic and political power. This perception resulted in wars becoming an even more vital aspect of public policy in a number of countries.

KEY WORDS CONTROL YOUR LIFE!

Among the first of these economic wars was the invasion and colonization of most of Southeast Asia and big chunks of China by European countries. In the early 1900s Japan joined the fray by invading and colonizing Korea.

Then came World War I and World War II, both started by Germany to expand its economic and political clout, with Japan soon following the German example by invading China, Southeast Asia and islands in the Pacific in the 1930's and 40's.

At present, most of the conflicts among industrialized nations are economic rather than military. But killing and other savage actions continue on a grand scale in some countries—despite efforts by the United Nations and individual nations to stop them.

No matter how many reasons one can come up with to explain this violence the ultimate cause lies in the lack of the right kind of practical and moral education; education that programs people in the commonsense attributes that are the foundation of peace, goodwill, tolerance and cooperation in improving the welfare of all—all things god-based religions have failed to do

There is virtually no area of human endeavor, including the survival and activities of religious institutions, that is not based on or does not depend on money. Technology could alter this dependence but that is a long way off, given the relationship between money, politics and power.

The first plague on humanity was/is the nature of males that has not yet evolved beyond the primitive id.

KEY WORDS CONTROL YOUR LIFE!

THE REAL GODS OF THE COSMOS!
The Nature of Nature!

Virtually all human beings were and still are totally ignorant of the size and nature of the universe and many people still credit the existence of all things to a creator god.

The truth is there are several Creator Gods!

The real creator gods of the universe are Hydrogen, Gravity and Dark Matter.

All of the 200 billion-plus stars in our own Milky Way galaxy are great balls of exploding Hydrogen atoms; as are all of the trillions of stars in the billions and billions of other galaxies in the universe.

The identity of what [who!] created the hydrogen-based stars is the greatest of all mysteries.

And it is not until stars age and die in massive explosions that they become the creator gods of all the solids and gases in the universe.

The exploding stars spew out trillions of tons of atoms that merge into all of the elements in the universe— water, planets, comets, asteroids, minerals and all known life forms.

This first water joined with great rocks of compressed dust to form comets, and over eons of time these rock-and-water comets not only brought water to planet Earth they also filled the oceans of water with the microbial ingredients that evolved into life forms.

KEY WORDS CONTROL YOUR LIFE!

In the human timeframe comets plunging into the Earth are exceedingly rare, so if you want to pray to a creator for whatever purpose, look up at the stars at night, select one of them, and address your prayers to it.

The second Creator God of the universe is Gravity, the power that controls the movement of the stars and all other solids and gases in the universe. It holds everything in its grasp in relation to all other matter in the universe, all of which move in predictable ways, depending on their gravitational pull in relation to other objects.

The third great God of the universe is known as Dark Matter.

Scientists say that it is Dark Matter that holds the billions of galaxies together as they move within the cosmos at fantastic speeds. They say that it makes up at least 25 percent of the matter of the universe, but they also say it cannot be seen or measured, making it the second greatest mystery of the universe.

So where in hell does all this leave us?

No wonder many people still put their faith in the little bitty mythical God first conceived by a primitive tribe of Jews about 6,000 years ago!!!

www.ingramcontent.com/pod-product-compliance
Lightning Source LLC
Chambersburg PA
CBHW051702170526
45167CB00002B/499